Praise for

Everything You Always Wanted to Know About God
(but were afraid to ask)

"Quick, witty, engaging, and often profound. These are words I use to describe my friend and one-time colleague Eric Metaxas. This little book is vintage Metaxas. Good and profitable reading."
—CHUCK COLSON, founder and chairman
of Prison Fellowship

"Eric Metaxas has written a book about God that is based on questions people are actually asking. His answers are pithy, practical, often funny (who says God doesn't have a sense of humor?), and true. This is a splendidly unconventional introduction to the Christian faith."
—JOHN WILSON, editor of Books and Culture

"An excellent primer on the most important questions of life, engagingly presented in question-and-answer format. A timely and useful book for a searching, spiritually hungry America."
—GEORGE GALLUP JR., founding chairman of the
George H. Gallup International Institute

"Finally, a book of apologetics you can give your friends without cringing!"
—LAUREN WINNER, author of *Girl Meets God*
and *Mudhouse Sabbath*

"Eric Metaxas takes you on a landmark tour of humanity's monumental questions in this handy hitchhikers' guide to God. Don't leave home without it."
—THOMAS GREANIAS, best-selling author of *Raising Atlantis*

"*Everything You Always Wanted to Know About God (but were afraid to ask)* doesn't intend to impress the reader; it speaks to the reader as a person would in a conversation. I've never encountered this subject dealt with so beautifully as it is dealt with here."

—BOB GRANT, host of *The Bob Grant Show* and author
of *Let's Be Heard*

"I am absolutely smitten with this book! It's fun to read but packed with good stuff to chew on. Every question in it I have asked, have heard asked, or want to ask! And the answers are so good-humored and easy to read that you almost forget how profound they are."

—ANN B. DAVIS, Alice of *The Brady Bunch*

"Rarely do a humorist, a logician, and an orthodox theological popularizer inhabit the same skin. So—quick, now!—join Eric Metaxas in this dialogue with skeptics, and let him deftly disabuse you of your vexing bewilderments."

—MCCANDLISH PHILLIPS, author and former
New York Times reporter

"To some, God is a stranger...and understandably so. Today's rumors and ignorance of God only deepen the mystery of his character. Metaxas makes it make sense. This clever and unswerving approach engages the intellectual and relaxes the skeptic. This book shows the real side of God—a God who wants us to have both quality and quantity of life."

—MAC MCNALLY, north Atlantic regional director of Young Life

"For his stylish and entertaining handling of this particular subject, Metaxas deserves a prize."

—DICK CAVETT, Emmy Award–winning television personality

EVERYTHING

YOU ALWAYS WANTED TO KNOW

ABOUT

GOD

(but were afraid to ask)

ERIC METAXAS

WATERBROOK
PRESS

EVERYTHING YOU ALWAYS WANTED TO KNOW ABOUT GOD (BUT WERE AFRAID TO ASK)
PUBLISHED BY WATERBROOK PRESS
12265 Oracle Boulevard, Suite 200
Colorado Springs, Colorado 80921
A division of Random House, Inc.

ISBN 1-4000-7101-1

Published in association with the literary division of Ambassador Agency, Nashville, Tennessee.

Library of Congress Cataloging-in-Publication Data
Metaxas, Eric.
    Everything you always wanted to know about God (but were afraid to ask) / Eric Metaxas.—1st ed.
        p. cm.
    Includes bibliographical references.
    ISBN 1-4000-7101-1
    1. God. I. Title.
BT103.M477 2005
231—dc22   2005016409

Printed in the United States of America
2005—First Edition

10 9 8 7 6 5 4 3 2 1

Feb. 6, 2008

To whom it may concern

To Martin —

(With gratitude.

God bless you.

Eric

Contents

Acknowledgments xi

Introduction 1

1   How Can You Prove God's Existence? 3
    The Meaning of "Proof"; What God Is Like; Miracles

2   Why Would a Loving God Allow Suffering? 19
    The Existence of Evil; Who's to Blame; God and Suffering

3   Does God *Really* Know Everything? 25
    What God Knows in Advance; How People Can Influence God

4   What's the Deal with Angels and Demons? 33
    Evidence for Both; The Difference Between the Two

5   What About the Paranormal and Life on Other Planets? . . . 43
    UFOs; Psychics; Reincarnation; Astrology; Wicca

6   Is God Against Us Having a Good Time? 57
    God and Sex; Sex and Marriage; God's View of Pleasure

7   Does God Hate Gays and Oppose Women? 65
    Hateful Christians; God and Gays; God's View of Women

8   Why Does Anyone Need Religion? 71
    Ritual and Superstition; God's Stance on Religion

9   Isn't One Religion About as Good as Another? 83
     How Religions Compare; Allah and God; The Meaning of Mercy

10   What's the *Real* Story on Adam and Eve? 95
     Forbidden Fruit; Falling from Grace; Made in God's Image

11   Does Hell Really Exist? 107
     What Hell Looks Like; Where It Is; Who Ends Up There

12   What About Heaven? 115
     What Happens When You Die; What Heaven Is;
     Who Ends Up There

13   Why Are Religious People Such Fanatics? 125
     Forms of Fanaticism; The Born-Again Thing;
     Christians in Your Face

14   How Can Anyone Take the Bible Seriously? 137
     Religious Texts; Dinosaurs; The Big Bang; Digging Archaeology

15   What Exactly Is Christianity? 157
     Religion Versus Relationship; Trust Versus Belief

16   What's the Point of Prayer? 165
     Unanswered Prayers; Faith and Prayer; Meditation and Prayer

17   What Does It Take to Believe in God? 173
     Faith and Reason; The Question of Meaning;
     The Definition of Trust

18   Who Says Jesus Is God's Son? 185
     Jesus as More than a Moral Teacher and a Great Role Model

19   Jesus Isn't *Really* the Only Way to God, Is He? 197
The Path to God; How God Reveals Himself

20   What Makes Conversion Real? 203
The True Meaning of "Conversion"; What Happens Afterward

Appendix: Recommended Reading 219
Notes 221

Acknowledgments

As John Milton might agree, justifying the ways of God to man can be something of a group effort. First of all I want to thank Father Peter Karloutsos of the Assumption Greek Orthodox Church in Danbury, Connecticut, who first encouraged me in the faith and instilled in me the confidence to continue asking questions. I also especially want to thank Ed Tuttle, a literal godsend, for giving me the model for this book. Over the course of many months some years ago, Ed tirelessly and lovingly was the "A" to my "Q" when I no longer believed that "A's" existed. I am eternally in his debt.

Finally, monster kudos to my agent and friend, Wes Yoder, for getting me an advance so huge I could finally afford to buy all those cable cars I've always wanted—what a mensch! Wait a minute! That was a dream. Alas! Still, Wes is a mensch. And, of course, lastly but certainly not leastly, I want to thank Ciccio (a.k.a. "Cheech") for aiding the creative process by "taking care of" the neighbors' annoyingly distracting Weimaraner, no questions "axed." [Note to self: remove this para from final.]

Introduction

Let's get one fact out of the way right off the bat. The very idea that someone would write a book with the title *Everything You Always Wanted to Know About God (but were afraid to ask)* is patently insane. And yet, here it is. And so the question, "Why?" Well, if there is an answer that might suffice, it's that almost everywhere I go I have conversations like the ones in this book. There is a palpable hunger for answers to these questions, but precious few places one might get them. So I did the only unreasonable thing a person might do under the circumstances: I took a crack at it. But perhaps that's the point. This is just that—a crack at it. This book is not meant (absurd title notwithstanding) to be definitive or exhaustive. I wanted it to be informal and conversational—to start a conversation that would go on far beyond these pages. I wanted to make the idea of a conversation on the subject of God inviting and, dare I say, even fun. I believe questions that are this serious not only require a little humor, they demand it. Maybe if we don't take these things too deadly seriously, we can actually learn something. As for the questions, if God can't take some hard questions thrown at him, then we have some really big problems. Call me crazy: I'm betting he can.

How Can You Prove God's Existence?

The Meaning of "Proof"; What God Is Like; Miracles

Sometime around 1890 a man and the young woman who would soon become his wife were walking in a field when the man saw an ant on the ground. He stooped down, let the ant crawl onto his index finger, and held it up for his fiancée to behold. (This was in the days before anyone had heard of Albert Einstein, so when someone wanted to refer to the Greatest Scientific Mind in Human History, they referred to Isaac Newton.) The man and woman looked at the ant, and then my great-grandfather spoke. "Tell Mr. Newton," he said, "to make me one of these."

Q: Let's cut to the chase: Does God exist?

A: Well, he certainly claims to.

Q: What do you mean "he claims to"? Isn't this a bit too serious to joke about?

A: Actually, no. In fact, it's too serious *not* to joke about. Wait, didn't I explain that in the introduction? I could have sworn…

Q: **Okay, but simply saying that God claims to exist doesn't do it for me. How can anyone prove that God exists when we can't see him? Isn't it something we just have to take on faith?**

A: You're bringing up a very important issue that comes up whenever anyone talks about God. The fact is that we live in a deeply materialistic culture. Our culture is so obsessed with the physical and the material that we have lost the ability to think logically about anything outside that realm.

> Our culture is so obsessed with the physical and the material that we have lost the ability to think logically about anything outside that realm.

Q: **What do you mean?**

A: Most folks know there is a realm beyond the physical, beyond our five senses. Remarkably few people would argue with that. But many people somehow believe there is no way to reasonably discuss anything outside the material realm, so they conclude that everyone can have whatever opinion they want on "spiritual" issues—which makes no sense. Because if there is such a thing as a spiritual reality, there's no reason it shouldn't be as solid as physical reality;

in some ways even *more* solid. And there's no reason we shouldn't be able to discuss it the same way we discuss anything else—like flying a plane or painting a landscape, or like physics. It's real. So it's subject to logic.

Q: Then it's possible to prove God exists?

A: Well, yes and no. This gets into the whole concept of what proof is. Yes, we can reason our way to God's existence. But no, we can't prove it definitively, the way we would a mathematical theorem. Actually, some philosophers *have* done that—they've come up with what they call "proofs of God's existence"—but most of us find such proofs dry and unconvincing. I certainly do. So let's first define what we mean by *proof.*

Q: Define away...

A: Sometimes we act as if proof has to be a black-and-white thing, but no one really believes that. We certainly don't act that way in our daily lives. For example, most parents know they love their children. But how would they prove it to a skeptic? It would be hard. But that doesn't mean their love is suspect.

Or think about this: I *know* electricity exists—and works. I have no doubt about it. But how could I prove it? I don't know enough about electricity to prove it, really, and yet there is no doubt in my mind that it is real and it works.

As a kid I once stuck my finger in a light socket...

Q: **Ouch!**

A: Exactly.

Q: **Anyway, your argument might hold water when it comes to parental love or electricity, but how does it prove there is a God?**

A: It doesn't. But it sets up the discussion so that we're not looking for the wrong kind of proof. It's important that we think logically and clearly about God. But we're still not going to approach the question of his existence the way we would a scientific experiment. His existence isn't demonstrable in the lab, but that doesn't mean that reason and common sense can't be applied to who and what God is.

We shouldn't check our brains at the door when we're dealing with issues of faith. We should think hard about these things and reason them out. But most folks feel that if something's not scientific or physical, then it can't be discussed rationally. They're mistaken. We must be rational and clear-minded when we're talking about the existence of God and about who he is. Anything else is really just superstition and mush.

Q: **Okay, let's be rational. How do we know God exists?**

A: The same way we know lots of things, such as whether someone loves us or whether electricity is real or just a crazy idea. We base our view of things, and our view of the world, on observation, including other people's observations. And we weigh the validity of other people's observations based on how trustworthy and credible those people are. So a number of things, taken together, form our view of everything, including God's existence and his nature. And it's on the basis of many different things that I know God does exist.

Q: You know he exists?

A: Yes. But again, I can't prove it to you in five minutes. It's a longer process than giving you a quick proof.

Q: What can you give me?

A: Well, in the course of this book, I can give you lots to chew on. But for the time being I can give you something fairly simple that would fall under the category of "the argument from design."

Q: What do you mean by that?

A: The argument for God from design basically says that the universe is so intricate and beautiful that it obviously didn't just happen; it *had* to have been designed by someone. If you find a watch on the ground, you know *someone* made that watch. You might not know who exactly, but you know it didn't just come into existence by accident. Ditto with Mount Rushmore, for example. You'd never look at it and say that it was a natural rock formation, that the wind and rain had carved out four faces over the millennia. You just know that someone was behind the design and creation of it.

Q: **You're stating the obvious. But what does this have to do with God?**

A: The same principle holds true with God and the world. The more you look at the universe and study it, the more it seems impossible that it all just happened by accident. Even many scientists who are not people of faith have come around to this way of thinking. It's simply not logical that it all just "happened," that no intelligence was behind it. Here is just one example of what I'm talking about, and please keep in mind that it doesn't "prove" anything. It's just a piece of information you need to think about in ultimately answering the bigger question.

Q: **Fire away.**

A: Okay, this might sound a bit odd, but think about the sizes of the sun and moon and their distances from Earth.

Q: **All right...**

A: As everyone will agree, the sun is about 93 million miles from the Earth. And the moon is about 240,000 miles from the Earth, or just less than a quarter of a million miles. You can get the exact figures and do the math yourself, but what it means, as your calculator will show, is that the distance from us to the sun is almost exactly four hundred times the distance from us to the moon.

Q: **I'm with you so far.**

A: Okay, here's where it gets weird. The *diameter* of the sun is almost exactly four hundred times the diameter of the moon.

Q: **You lost me. Meaning?**

A: Meaning that because of this, when you look at them
from our vantage point—from the Earth—they look
exactly the same size. Not *sort of* the same size, but *exactly*
the same size.

   If you were designing a planet with a sun and moon in
the sky, wouldn't it be nice to get them to look *exactly* the
same size, just for the symmetry and aesthetics of it, even
though they are millions of miles apart and gigantically different in size from each other? The whole thing is all the
more astonishing when you see that other planets and their
moons don't begin to come anywhere close to this. Not one
of them does.

   Our moon is about fifteen hundred miles across, but
the moons of Mars are nine and seventeen miles across.
They're a couple of glorified boulders compared to our
moon. You wonder that they are even called moons. Not
only that, but most planets have several moons. Jupiter has
twelve. But only our planet has this mind-boggling, once-
in-a-solar-system super-symmetry, one moon and one sun
that—to us—look precisely the same size.

Q: **That really is a bit odd.**

A: It's nuts. Of course it *could* be pure happenstance, but what
are the odds of that? And one of the results of this extraordinary fact is that we have eclipses. The moon and the
Earth have to fit precisely over each other for *total* eclipses
to occur. But they do happen, almost as if it has all been
planned for our benefit. Again, this doesn't *prove* anything,

but to an unbiased and open mind, it can't be anything less than astonishing.

Q: Okay, for now let's say that God exists. But if he exists, what's he like?

A: He likes walks in the rain…fluffy pillows…quiet candlelit dinners…

Q: Very funny. I didn't mean what <u>does</u> he like; I meant what <u>is</u> he like?

A: Sorry. I couldn't resist.

Q: For example, is he some remote higher being or energy force, or is he, as I've heard it said, a "person"?

A: Well, he *is* a higher being—the *highest,* in fact. And yes, he's also a person. But before we go too far with this, understand that many people have an odd idea that God is an old man with a white beard sitting on a cloud. That's not God; it's just our imaginations at work. But on some important level, God is a person. What's really important to think about is that God is not some vague, impersonal energy force or some dispassionate Creator who is "all Mind" or something like that. That's a recent New Age concept, not a biblical one. If there is one thing God has made clear in the Bible, it's that he is a person and that we are persons because he made us in his own image.

Q: But why is it so important that God is a "person"?

A: Because it radically affects how we see him. If we think of God as a being like us, we know that he understands us and isn't just some ethereal brain or energy field that doesn't particularly care if we live or die. We also know that God has a personality, that he thinks and reasons and communicates with us in a way that is on some level similar to the way another human would do so.

Q: Okay, if God is a person, is God male or female?

A: That's a tough one to answer. We know that when Jesus prayed, he addressed God as his Father. And when Jesus' disciples asked him to teach them how to pray, he told them to pray to their Father in heaven.

Q: So you're saying God is male?

A: Not exactly. Because we also know that when God created us in his image, the Bible says, "male and female He created them."[1] Which would lead you to believe that God is somehow both male and female.

Q: So what's the right answer?

A: I think this is one of those questions that doesn't have a "right" answer. We know that Jesus taught his followers to talk to "God our Father." And there is no question that when Christians pray to Jesus, they are praying to someone who was a man while he was on earth. But there are a few places in the Bible where God uses metaphors to lead us to

believe that he has maternal and mothering qualities, too. I
think it's safest to pray to him as our Father in heaven and
to think of him that way because Jesus did. But we all need
to keep the perspective that God has *both* male and female
qualities, and that's why he made us male and female.

Q: **Okay, how about this? If God is a person, does he
have a sense of humor?**
A: Wouldn't he have to?

Q: **I don't know. I'm asking you.**
A: God created everything that's good, so he'd have to have
invented humor, which is obviously good (though, like all
good things, it can be used to hurt and harm as well). And
when you consider that he created us in his image, it seems
that because we have a sense of humor, he'd have to have
one as well. Self-consciousness—or self-awareness—leads,
among other things, to humor, doesn't it?

Q: **I don't know, does it?**
A: Yes, and since God created us with self-consciousness, he
created us with an ability to understand such things as irony
and sarcasm. (Jesus had moments when he was short and
sometimes even sarcastic with people—his disciples and
Jewish religious leaders alike. I don't know how else to read
some of the passages in the New Testament.[2]) Anyone who
is reasonably emotionally healthy has a sense of humor, so it
seems that God would have to have a sense of humor too.
Or some semblance of one.

Q: What about miracles? How can any reasonable person believe in them?

A: Good question. Here's one answer: If we believe—as many scientists do—that God created the world, that he created the entire universe and everything in it—including quasars and black holes and Saturn and the Grand Canyon and thunder and lightning and whales and hummingbirds and fleas and you and me—and that he created it all in an instant from something 10 trillion times smaller than the period at the end of this paragraph, it doesn't seem like a big deal to make the leap that he could do relatively easy things like parting the Red Sea or healing lepers, does it? It's kind of like accepting that Tolstoy wrote *War and Peace* but then being shocked that he could move a comma in the manuscript.

Q: Okay, let's assume for the moment that God _can_ do miracles. Why would he want to violate the rules he had already set up? It's like admitting that the rules weren't all that hot in the first place, so every once in a while he has to cheat to make things come out the way he wants them to.

A: Good point. Still, there are a number of reasons God might violate his own rules. But what's to say he actually does? We sometimes assume we know all the rules with the little bit of science we have. But any of the scientists living in the nineteenth century who knew everything about Newtonian physics would have been blown away by the concepts of relativity and quantum physics. They would have said that one particle affecting another particle in another part of the universe—which is what quantum physics teaches—is impossible, a miracle. But today we know it's just science.

Q: Okay, but are you saying that God would <u>never</u> violate his nature or break his own laws, that every single miracle is somehow natural?

A: Well, again, you'd have to define *natural,* and that's not so easy to do. When someone is miraculously healed and science can't explain it, does the fact that it is perhaps supernatural also mean that is isn't on some level *natural?* Isn't it possible that God is working within the rules he set up, but in a way that we can't understand? Isn't it possible that our knowledge of the natural world is incredibly limited?

Q: I suppose so...

A: I mean, you at least have to think about that sort of thing. It's important not to leap to conclusions. Human beings love to assume that everything they know is all that can be known—which, of course, is a mistake.

Q: Are there some miracles God can do and some he can't?

A: Yes. The best way to explain this would be by telling you a
    story. A few years ago I was writing my own adaptation of a
    Grimm's fairy tale, and in the process I decided to see what
    the original German version said. The fairy tale is about a
    talking fish that grants a fisherman and his overly ambitious
    wife every imaginable wish. When the fisherman's wife says
    she wants to live in a vast castle and be the empress of the
    world, the fish grants her wish. And we suddenly find her
    sitting on a throne that every version of the story says is two
    miles high! That's right, two miles.

    Somehow, immediately you know that something is
    wrong. I mean, the Empire State Building is a quarter of a
    mile high! Even in a story with a talking fish, you know
    there can't be a throne two miles high. You'd die of a heart
    attack sitting on a throne like that. But there in the original
    German version, it used the word *myle,* which means mile.
    But somehow I knew this couldn't be right—it didn't *feel*
    right. So with a little research I found that the German
    word *myle* also has another definition, a much older one.
    The archaic definition of *myle* is "fathom," which is about
    fifteen feet.

    "Aha," said I. "So the throne was thirty feet high, not
    ten thousand feet high!" Thirty feet is high enough for a
    high throne, don't you think?

Q: I suppose so.

A: But the bigger question is, "How did I know that the
    throne couldn't be two miles high?"

Q: Okay, I'll take the bait. How did you know?

A: It has something to do with the internal logic and rules of the story. In this fantastical and wonderful story, many details seem appropriately fantastical and wonderful, like the talking fish. But the detail of a throne that was two miles high didn't seem fantastical and wonderful; it just seemed ridiculous and wrong. It stopped the story cold.

Q: What does this have to do with God not being able to perform certain miracles?

A: Everything. What I'm saying is that once an author creates something, it begins to have a logic and nature of its own. As the reader, you don't think to yourself, *Well, absolutely* anything *can happen.* On the contrary, while you give the author lots of leeway to do what he or she likes, there are boundaries and limits to what you will accept. And in the talking-fish fairy tale, the two-mile-high throne was far beyond that limit. That's because once the creator or author has established the unwritten rules, even he is not free to write anything he wants. So if in this story the author has written "two miles" instead of "thirty feet," something in the reader says, "Wait a minute, that's wrong. That violates the rules of this story." Which shows that an author submits to the internal rules he has set down from the beginning. And, of course, in the case of the fairy tale with the talking fish, it wasn't the author who screwed up, it was a bad translator.

Q: So? My question was about God not being able to perform some miracles.

A: Right. So when God created the universe, he created it in a way that precludes even him from monkeying with certain aspects of it. He laid out certain ground rules, just as anyone does when he or she is creating anything. It's part of the warp and woof of creation itself. Every creation has a kind of internal order. God has allowed himself all kinds of leeway, but there are limits in his creation that even he respects and stays within—and he designed it that way. To go beyond the limits is to violate his own nature as well as the nature of the creation. So God allows himself to do almost anything, but he cannot and will not do something that is the equivalent of sticking a two-mile-high throne in a story where it is patently out of place. You might find all kinds of amazing things, but some things you will not find.

Q: **Can you give me an example?**

A: Well, you might find God parting the Red Sea so the Hebrew slaves could escape their captors in Egypt, or you might find him healing someone miraculously, but you will never find God doing something that is not within his nature. For example, he will not lie or deceive or do something tricky and confusing. Ever. And he won't do something that violently violates the fundamental rules of his creation.

So what might seem to be a contradiction—that God is actually limited rather than being all-powerful—is really a tremendous truth about God. Namely, that God limits himself precisely because he *is* all-powerful. He decides what is and isn't, what can and can't be done, and he always remains true to his nature. This is no contradiction; it's simply God operating fully within his nature. He can do any miracle that is consistent with his nature, but he will not do a miracle that would violate it.

My great-grandfather was not a religious man. He was an intellectual, somewhat famous in his day. But he knew that the mysterious Creator of the universe—whoever he was and wherever he was—sometimes left bits of evidence for us to stumble across if we walked slowly enough and if we had our eyes open. Some of those bits of evidence are actually quite small; sometimes they are no larger than an ant.

2

Why Would a Loving God Allow Suffering?

The Existence of Evil; Who's to Blame; God and Suffering

On a historic spring day in 1947, Jackie Robinson, wearing a Brooklyn Dodgers uniform, became the first black man to play in a major league baseball game. At the time many felt elation that the color barrier in baseball had finally been broken, but others felt deep hatred for Robinson and all he seemed to represent. It would not be an easy season.

But Branch Rickey, the Dodgers' general manager, was a canny fellow. He knew that breaking the color barrier would take far more than a .300 hitter who could steal bases. The player he chose would have to be able to stand up to something even more intimidating than the best fastball pitchers in the world. The man he chose would have to face slurs and personal insults worse than anything he'd experienced before. Crowds would scream their hatred at him; other players would call him unprintable names. Rickey knew that if the player he chose fought back, the cause would be set back a decade or more. But what man could resist the temptation to fight back?

Rickey, who was a devout Christian, sought out an athlete who was a similarly devout Christian, someone who could be persuaded to turn the other cheek. That was Jesus' way of dealing with evil, and it was what he commanded his followers to do. Such an approach would make absolutely no sense to most athletes. It would seem cowardly. But Rickey knew that if the man he chose agreed to obey God's command, the evil of racial hatred in major league baseball could eventually be defeated. And so he chose Jackie Robinson. The rest is civil rights history.

Q: **What is evil?**

A: Evil is that which is utterly opposed to God and, consequently, utterly opposed to all that is good, loving, beautiful, kind, true, and so on.

Q: **But the various understandings of evil are so subjective. Who's to say what really is evil and what is just a matter of personal preference or belief?**

A: Let me say, first, that the idea that evil exists makes many people very uncomfortable, and in some cases, it frightens them. But for many the idea of evil simply strikes them as moralistic and old-fashioned. And yet who would deny that Hitler and those who served him were conduits for evil? What other term could we use to describe what happened under his regime? Or during Stalin's and Pol Pot's dictatorships?

The main reason the term *evil* makes some of us

squirm is because it implies a black-and-white moral order, which means that we have to deal with that moral order and how our own behavior fits into it. And yes, we all have to deal with it. Sometimes people will try to avoid the issue by saying something like, "Well, that's evil from *your* point of view."

Q: Exactly. That's what I was saying before.

A: But is that because the idea of *objective* evil seems too harsh? A lot of people can't deal with the idea that something could be objectively evil, because for something to be objectively evil implies a certain someone—God—who is objectively *good.* It implies a moral standard outside ourselves. But just because we don't like the idea of a set moral standard doesn't make evil go away. It's real, and we need to see it for what it is.

Q: But if there is such a thing as evil and if there is a God who is good, why would this supposedly good God create a world with so much evil and suffering in it?

A: You may already know it, but this is *the* classic question, and many books have been written on the subject. The best is Peter Kreeft's *Making Sense Out of Suffering,* which is a must-read if you haven't already read it.

On the question of God and suffering, there is no completely satisfactory answer. With some questions, we can sort of bite right into the center of an answer and get the full and satisfying taste and texture of it. But other times we can only nibble around the edges of the answer and hope to catch most of its flavor and get a few good hints at what it is ultimately like. The question of why God allows suffering is definitely one of the latter.

Q: Can you at least try to answer it?

A: Sure. Evil is not caused by God, and it doesn't come from God. But God allows evil to exist because he gave us all free will, and he wants us to exercise that will. It would be meaningless to have the ability to make choices if there were only one option available—if, for example, there were only good in the universe. For us to be able to either choose God or reject him, there has to be an option B. And in this case, option B is everything God is not—namely evil.

Let's look at it another way: God created us out of love, and he wants us to love him back. But love can never be forced. We can love our kids so much that it hurts, but we can never force them to love us in return. It's the same with God. He can't force us to love him.

Love, by definition, is always freely given. So God, in order to make it possible for us to love him, gave us free will. Which means we can also choose *not* to love him. By giving us free will, God gave us the ability to reject him and all that is good, and thereby bring evil into our world. And all of us suffer in this life because of the evil that exists.

> By giving us free will, God gave us the ability to reject him and all that is good, and thereby bring evil into our world.

Q: So you believe that, somehow, humanity <u>chose</u> to endure all this suffering?

A: Think about this: God could perhaps have created us as some form of robotic creatures who were forced to love him and accept his authority over us. But in God's infinite wisdom, he didn't. Again, we can't understand it completely—at least not right now. The best we can do is to see that if our kids loved us because they had to, it wouldn't be love. There is something about love and free will that is part of the grand nature of things.

Free will makes love possible because love is always voluntary. But the other side of free will is that we also have the option to blow it, and…well…at one point we sort of blew it big time.

Q: What do you mean by that?

A: I'm referring to the Garden of Eden and the Fall, which we can get into later because that brings up its own wacky set of questions. But the fact is that at some point in the dawn of our history, the first humans chose to exercise their option. They rejected God, and by making that choice, they allowed all of the negatives that come with that decision into the world we inhabit. Hence sin, death, evil—you name it; if it's bad we let it in.

Q: But why would God create a world where these things could get in? Seems to me like he really messed up.

A: You certainly have to wonder. Still, it's not God who allowed these things into his creation any more than a mom and dad allow drugs to be stashed in their teenager's room. It's just that when you are dealing with human beings and not robots, you get a lot of bad with the good. But again, the free will to choose the bad is what gives meaning to choosing the good. We choose in favor of one thing and against another.

This is not anything like a deeply satisfying answer, I know. The fact is that the question of human suffering bumps right up against the very mystery of life itself. It's about as big as questions get, and people who try to give you a pat answer are kidding you and themselves both.

Jackie Robinson's response to the evil and hatred that came against him in the summer of 1947 was nothing less than heroic. God calls us to be heroic in the face of evil. He knows that suffering isn't easy, yet he doesn't promise to take the suffering away, at least in this life. But God does promise to be with us in our suffering.

Every night of that historic summer, Jackie Robinson would kneel by his bed and pray that the God who had commanded him to turn the other cheek in the face of evil would comfort him in his suffering and would give him the strength to continue. Robinson knew it wasn't possible by human means alone. But he also knew that with God, all things are possible.

3

Does God *Really* Know Everything?

What God Knows in Advance; How People Can Influence God

Have you ever wondered what would happen if someone succeeded in creating a time machine? What would happen if you could actually go back in time? And what would happen if, while you were back there, you got swept up in a historic event, like a war, and killed an enemy combatant who turned out to be one of your ancestors? Would that mean you'd never be born?

But wait, if you'd never been born, who was it that traveled back in time and killed your ancestor? When you step outside the normal constraints of time, things immediately get very complicated.

Q: It is often said that God knows everything that's going to happen before it happens. If that's true, then it really doesn't matter what we do, does it?

A: Your question presupposes that God exists in a space-time continuum similar to the world we live in.

Q: **Pardon me?**
A: God is outside of time. He's outside time *and* space, to be perfectly accurate.

Q: **What does that have to do with God knowing in advance everything that's going to happen?**
A: The point is that God is not limited by space or time. He is simultaneously everywhere at once. And he knows everything there is to know. So God knowing something in advance is true from our time-bound perspective, since the thing hasn't happened yet in our world. But to God, knowing everything at once is just part of being God. I know it's a bit crazy.

Q: **Okay, so God knows everything. My real question is this: If God is going to do what he wants to anyway, it's not as if I can do anything to change his mind, can I?**
A: First of all, just because God knows everything doesn't mean that he *determines* everything. Big difference. He might know that when you roll the dice, it'll come up boxcars, but that doesn't mean he made it happen. Just because God knows everything that will happen doesn't mean he *makes* it happen. Things are not predetermined and fatalistic. Chance is often involved, and our free will is often involved, right?

Q: **I suppose...**

A: This is a very important concept. God gave us free will. He might know the day and hour you are going to die, but it doesn't mean he *chose* the exact time or day of your death.

Q: **Really?**

A: Really. You have free will. So you could drink yourself to death or jump off a bridge, but neither of these events is God's will. He might know what you are going to do and when, but he might also be dead set against it.

> Just because God knows everything that will happen doesn't mean he makes it happen.

Q: **This is deep.**

A: I told you.

Q: **Then why do so many people say things like "When your number's up, your number's up" or "You're gonna go when you're gonna go"?**

A: They're just repeating something they've heard, but it is absolutely not true. Not if the Bible and five thousand years of belief in the God of the Bible have anything to say to us.

Q: **You're sure about this?**

A: Absolutely. Think about it. If I freak out and kill ten innocent people, and then the cops close in, and I kill two of them and then kill myself, do you think that was something

God did? Do you think that was his plan for my life and the lives of the dozen people who just got killed? Do you think God, who loves us and wants the best for us, would sign off on that?

Q: So you're saying that God <u>does</u> know everything in advance, but that he's not responsible for the bad things that happen.

A: Exactly. Just because God allows evil and sin does *not* mean he is the force behind them. That's an extremely important distinction. God is the strongest opponent of evil, but he doesn't force his will on us. It's up to us to choose to live according to his desires. He may know what we are going to do, but that doesn't mean he approves of it or makes it happen. God is doing everything he can to get us to make the right choices, but he won't force us.

We aren't clockwork automatons who simply act out some pre-scripted roles that have been assigned to us. Instead, God effectively created us as actors who can improvise and make up part of the story along with him, the Author. So on some level we are characters in God's book, in his story, but he has created us as characters who are also co-creators. Think of it: We are characters in God's story, and on some level we get to participate in aspects of the writing! That's like Romeo or Juliet getting a cowriting credit with Shakespeare. Or like Ebenezer Scrooge or Bob Cratchit making suggestions and edits on Charles Dickens's *A Christmas Carol.* The implications are awesome!

Q: Okay, what are the implications for us?

A: For one thing, it shows that God is amazing because he can
create characters who are fully autonomous moral beings—
us. We have free will and are involved in his creation and
his story right alongside him. He has given us a measure of
power and freedom that is really overwhelming and startling. I mean, if I were God, I don't think I would have
done that. I wouldn't risk my whole creation and all of history and eternity on a planet of folks like us. Why risk
doing that when you could instead have simply created a
planet full of creatures who do exactly what you want them
to do and get it right every time?

Q: Exactly. What's up with that?

A: That's the mystery. Despite the fact that he was giving
humans the capacity to break his heart—which we did
many times and continue to do—he still gave us that freedom. That's really at the core of who God is.

Q: But if God already knows everything, why does he
need anyone to pray? I don't get that.

A: Well, it's not that he *needs* us to pray. He allows us to pray.
He lets us participate in the process of making bad things
turn good. Humans can enter the process of redemption
alongside God. Honestly, this is a huge and frightening
privilege when you think about it. Mere mortals have a

chance to pray for justice and for the triumph of good over evil, among other things.

God's original intention was never that there should be disease and suffering and injustice and death. Because of the Fall (Adam and Eve rebelling and eating the forbidden fruit), everything is royally messed up, but through doing God's will and through prayer, we are able to begin to bring God's will to bear on various situations. We have a chance to bring the beauty and order and love and justice and grace of the kingdom of God into a hurting and disordered world. That's God's will, and he has given his followers the daunting job of being a meaningful part of how he brings these things to pass.

Remember, God designed the universe in such a way that we have an active role in it. Everything is not predetermined. God has given us the freedom to affect things, through our actions and through prayers to him, when we ask him to act.

Q: But won't God do what he has already decided to do, whether or not people pray?

A: He can do that, of course, but for some reason he chooses to act on certain things only after he is asked. Go figure. There are many examples of this in the Bible. When Abraham asked God to spare Sodom and Gomorrah, for example, God reconsidered his decision and entered into a long negotiating session with Abraham. When Moses pleaded with God to spare the idol-worshiping Israelites, God listened to Moses' argument and held back his judgment.[1] We still don't know why God wants us to get involved, but somehow he does.

Q: **What's your theory? Why does God want people to pray and get involved?**

A: There are several theories. One that makes a lot of sense is that through prayer, we ourselves are changed. By talking to God, we find that our attitudes and feelings change. Through prayer we begin to see things from God's perspective, which helps us get in tune with his plans. So it's sometimes about prayer changing *us* more than it is about us trying to get God to do something we want.

Another theory is that God created us to participate in bringing about his will on earth, and prayer is one of the main ways we do that. The bottom line is he does want us to pray. It makes a difference in the outcome of events— even though God really does know everything in advance.

God is outside of time entirely. Having created time, he stands apart from it. The very idea that God, who is outside time, somehow entered time by sending his Son, Jesus, into our world is a profound mystery. But it is no less a mystery that we have a God-given ability to pray to the God who exists outside of time so that he might affect things that are within our world of time.

What's the Deal with Angels and Demons?

Evidence for Both; The Difference Between the Two

Twenty years ago theologian Walter Wink wrote the following passage, which today rings as true, if not truer, than when he wrote it:

> What does late twentieth-century Western society exclude from conversation? Certainly not sex; at least in more "sophisticated" circles, accounts of sexual exploits scarcely raise an eyebrow. But if you want to bring all talk to a halt in shocked embarrassment, every eye riveted on you, try mentioning angels, or demons, or the devil. You will be quickly appraised for signs of pathological violence and then quietly shunned. [These things], along with all other spiritual realities, are the unmentionables of our culture.[1]

Q: The whole concept of angels and demons sounds so
medieval. Isn't believing in them today sort of like
believing in elves and unicorns?

A: Perhaps. But there's one big difference. Elves and unicorns
don't actually exist. Angels and demons *do*.

Q: That's it? Your answer is "they exist"?

A: Basically, yes. Jesus himself referred to them as existing. And
through the ages thousands of people have testified to their
existence. But it's hard for us to accept this idea because we
have very strong preconceived cultural notions about reality.
We live in a culture that is emphatically, obsessively materi-
alist. We've been pretty well brainwashed. So the question
isn't, "Does this other reality exist?" It does. The real question is, "What's it like?"

Remember that not too many years ago we didn't know
anything about quantum physics or subatomic particles.
Now we do. We are bumping up against some stuff that is a
bit beyond what we are used to, and we have to be able to
deal with that without flatly saying it doesn't exist. Besides,
not to be cheeky, but doesn't it seem that those people who
are so positive God doesn't exist don't really want him to
exist, so as not to interfere with the way they live their lives?

Q: What?

A: Don't we at least have to factor that into the whole equation? That a lot of the people who say that God and the
spiritual realm can't exist desperately *hope* God doesn't exist?
Why would someone want to kill the conversation so

emphatically despite all of the evidence and experience to the contrary? And how can they be so *sure* God doesn't exist? Aren't they being a little simplistic and reductive? If you can't prove he does, you can't prove he doesn't, right?

> The question isn't, "Does this other reality exist?"
> It does. The real question is, "What's it like?"

Q: **But what does that have to do with angels and demons?**

A: The point is that there is ample evidence for the existence of angels and demons. But you're never going to find a mummified angel carcass in a museum, if that's the sort of proof you're looking for. And you're never going to find a scaly demon claw floating in a jar of formaldehyde in a lab. But millions of people have had experiences that, taken together, add up to a rather extraordinary body of evidence. Let's just say that you can't entirely discount it. To do so is to be intellectually dishonest and perhaps even a little closed-minded. You can't read a book like Malachi Martin's *Hostage to the Devil* or M. Scott Peck's *People of the Lie* and say there is nothing to the whole subject of demons. Or for a book that's even more convincing, read M. Scott Peck's *Glimpses of the Devil.* It's chilling.

Q: **If demons do in fact exist—and I'm not saying they do—what exactly are they?**

A: Demons are fallen angels. In other words, God created vast
    numbers of angels, and the best theology on this subject
    says that one-third of them chose to follow Satan, who was
    the first fallen angel.[2] All of this seems to have happened in
    some past eternity when angels still had the freedom to
    choose whom they would follow—God or Satan. It doesn't
    seem that they have free will anymore, so now angels are
    somehow incapable of not following God's will, and demons
    are incapable of reversing their earlier decision to side with
    Satan.

    What a horrible thought. Their decisions were cast for
    all eternity. Our decisions are cast for eternity too, but while
    we're here on earth, we can still choose to open ourselves to
    receive God's love, or we can choose to close ourselves off
    from that love. We can always rethink our choices and
    reverse direction. But once we leave this planet, our choice
    has been made, and either we join the angels for eternity...
    or we don't.

Q: **Why would angels choose to rebel against God?**
A: This is another big mystery, and to pretend to fully under-
    stand it is to kid ourselves. But we can begin to understand
    it by wondering why human beings—you or I—would
    choose to rebel against God. Sometimes we just want our
    own way, and we don't trust the one who is most trust-
    worthy of all. It doesn't make sense, but we all do it at
    some time—and some people never stop doing it.

Q: **I'm feeling the need for a bit more backstory...**

A: Well, as the story goes, the lead archangel, who was the most glorious being God had ever created, decided that he was wonderful enough to go it alone, without God around to steal his limelight, so to speak. I think you could say that he fell in love with himself. And fell hard.

Q: So now he's fallen and can't get up?

A: Something like that. And let's not kid ourselves; he really was glorious. But he forgot that it was God who made him that way. Instead of being grateful for what God had given him, this archangel chose to take it all for himself, apart from God. The way John Milton famously put it in his epic poem *Paradise Lost* is that it seemed to him far preferable to "reign in hell, than serve in heaven."[3]

The archangel wanted to be the star of his own show, even if it meant turning his back on all that is good and glorious and beautiful. Of course, humans are inclined to do that as well. Except we often don't know we are doing it when we do it. It can be subtle. It always makes me think of that amazing Pink Floyd line, "And did you exchange a walk-on part in the war for a lead role in a cage?"[4]

Sometimes we do the same thing Satan did when he chose to lead the eternally losing side rather than serve as a top lieutenant to God on the eternally winning side. He couldn't stand not being in charge.

Q: But isn't it natural to want to be in charge?

A: It's perfectly natural. But that doesn't mean it's in our best interest. It's really a matter of pride. Many theologians have called pride the number-one sin because it's the sin that leads to all the other sins. We're too proud to bow down to God, too proud to say we're wrong. Of course, we're not talking about pride in the good sense, as in "I'm proud of my daughter" or "I'm proud of my hard work and accomplishments." We're talking about the bad and classical sense of pride. We're talking about self-aggrandizing pride, pride that puts oneself first, ahead of everyone else. This is the pride that leads to a fall, as the Bible says.[5] In this case, that's exactly what happened, big time: Satan's pride led him—and us—to *the* Fall.

Q: And you're saying that demons are former angels who chose to follow him?

A: Yes. Not the swiftest move, eh?

Q: Can we change the subject to angels? You say they exist, but what are they exactly?

A: It helps to know what the word *angel* means. It's derived from a Greek word *angelos,* which means "messenger." So angels are simply God's messengers.

Q: I still find it hard to swallow the idea that angels exist.

A: Just because we usually can't see them, we shouldn't assume they don't exist. The spiritual realm is just as "real" as the physical realm.

Q: So if angels are God's messengers, as you say, then
what about praying to them?

A: Not a good idea.

Q: Why not?

A: God wants us to pray to him only, and angels are not him.
They're his creatures, just as we're his creatures. We're not
supposed to pray to creatures; we're supposed to pray to the
Creator.

Q: Then why do some people do it?

A: A few reasons. For one thing, anything that seems more
beautiful, more holy, or above us in any way tends to create
in us the feeling of awe—which is the same reason some
people pray to nature or to Mother Earth. But all of these
created things are only reflections of the beauty and holiness
and awesomeness of the one who created them. So to worship them is wrong. It is misplaced affection. God is very
clear that we are to worship him alone. You've heard the
phrase "Don't shoot the messenger"?

Q: Yeah.

A: Well, we shouldn't worship the messenger either. And angels
are just that, messengers.

Q: But what about people who find that their prayers
to angels get answered?

A: Just because someone answers your prayers doesn't mean
that that someone has your best interests in mind. The

Bible says very clearly that Satan always disguises himself as an angel of light. He never announces himself for who he really is. Jesus calls him the father of all lies.[6] So Satan isn't about to come out and tell us, "I'm Satan, the source of all disease and death and mayhem and pain and suffering and injustice. Follow me!" On the contrary, he presents himself as someone good, someone who means to help us. But because he is perfectly evil, the exact opposite is true. We have to really know who God is, or Satan will fool us.

It's just like the pimp who buys a hamburger for a sixteen-year-old runaway when she hasn't eaten in days and gives her a place to sleep and some nice clothes. It's definitely not because he has her best interests in mind. He only has *his* best interests in mind, and he will use her and abuse her. But he presents himself as someone who is there to help. Satan's just like that. The pimp wants to own the girl just as Satan wants to own us.

Q: You're saying that angels who answer certain prayers are angels who follow Satan?

A: Well, they're not really angels anymore; they're demons. But they present themselves as angels.

Q: So you believe that people who pray to angels are actually praying to demons?

A: Ghastly as that might sound, yes. People who pray to angels are deluded, and Satan will continue to delude them into believing in anything or anyone—including "angel guides" or "spirit guides" or what have you—as long as he can keep people from turning to the one true God. That's Satan for you. Not exactly a nice guy. But we knew that.

Human beings tend to want to tame the things that frighten them. And so we have television shows that make demons seem like manageable problems, things we can deal with through superior magic, and sometimes a little kick boxing. And angels, far from being the awesome creatures that make grown men and women in the Bible fall on their knees in terror, are depicted as smiling cherubs with pink cheeks. This is all fine if demons and angels don't actually exist—but what if they do?

What About the Paranormal and Life on Other Planets?

UFOs; Psychics; Reincarnation; Astrology; Wicca

When I was growing up in the 1970s, it seemed that every time I turned on a television talk show, I'd see astrologers, hypnotists, spoon-bending psychics, people who claimed to talk to the dead, and others who said they had encountered aliens—not to mention Bigfoot. As Johnny Carson used to say, "Wild and wacky stuff." Spirituality was everywhere, but rarely did I see anything about the kind of spirituality I'd experienced in church.

If there is a spirit world, it can't be whatever we want it to be. It is what it is, which raises the question, "What exactly is it like?"

Q: There are a lot of things that are unseen and that no one can seem to explain. For example, what does the Bible say about psychics and ESP?

A: Nothing good. The Bible doesn't deny the existence of psychic power, as some folks do. It says there are indeed such things as paranormal powers and that they are all too real. But they are emphatically not from God, so we should be very careful of them. In fact, we should avoid them entirely. Folks who traffic in this stuff are playing with fire and usually don't know it—till they get burned, so to speak.

Q: **If these supernatural powers aren't bogus, then what exactly are they?**

A: Well, there's no use beating around the bush. They're demonic.

Q: **Here we go again. Isn't talking about the devil and demons just a way of using scare tactics on people?**

A: Well, it's only scare tactics if it's not true. If someone says to a kid, "Don't play out in the road because you might get hit by a car," and the child says, "That's a scare tactic," you'd say that (a) it's not a scare tactic, and (b) this kid stands a good chance of getting hit by a car.

Just because people have twisted and abused a concept—in this case, Satan and demons—doesn't mean that the original concept isn't valid. Just because we've had absurd images of a guy in a red suit and a pitchfork foisted on us doesn't mean we have to accept those absurd images. But the concept of Satan, which is derived from a Hebrew word meaning "adversary," is a concept that is right at the heart of how the Bible has always portrayed things. Satan tempted Adam and Eve, Satan tempted Jesus, and Satan or his minions tempt us today. Nothing is crazy about that. It's just an invisible reality, but since it's invisible, it's very easy to pervert and bend it out of all recognizable shape. Besides, as I said earlier, most people in our society rule out the possibility of things existing outside the material world. But those things in the spirit realm haven't lost sight of us.

Q: **Spooky. Where do you get these ideas?**

A: I get them from the Bible and from two thousand years of Christian tradition. Saint Peter warned the followers of Jesus that Satan "walks about like a roaring lion, seeking whom he may devour."[1] Jesus pointed out to Peter that Satan wanted to "sift" him like wheat, meaning that Satan wanted to test the disciple's faith.[2] Jesus never made any special point of proving the existence of Satan; he simply assumed it, as did his disciples. And just as the word *Satan* comes from the Hebrew word for "adversary,"[3] so *devil* is the English equivalent for the Hebrew word for "accuser,"[4] because one of the main things Satan does is accuse us of our sins. Anytime someone is taking delight in accusing you or anyone else of sins, you can be sure that person isn't being motivated by God.

Q: **As long as we're talking about the spirit realm, what does the Bible say about talking to the dead?**

A: It says you should talk very loudly, because the first thing that goes when you're dead is your hearing.

Q: Hello?

A: Sorry, I couldn't resist. Seriously, the Bible says we shouldn't talk to the dead. The Old Testament word for this is *necromancy,* and God always lumps necromancy in with sorcery and all of the other prohibited occultic stuff. The idea is that if we open ourselves up to this sort of thing, we are opening ourselves up to the dark realm, and that is something we definitely do not want to do.

> When talking to the dead, you should talk very loudly, because the first thing that goes when you're dead is your hearing.

Q: But what about séances? What harm could there be in a widow talking to her dead husband?

A: It's not a matter of a widow getting in touch with her dead husband; it's a matter of talking to spirits who are not of God. And as I've said before, anything that is not of God is something to avoid. Like the use of a Ouija board, which many consider to be simply an entertaining party game. If only they knew…

Q: You're saying Ouija boards are dangerous? You've got to be kidding.

A: There's no question that Ouija boards are dangerous, *very* dangerous. Have you seen *The Exorcist*?

Q: Why do you ask?

A: Well, I don't recommend that you go out and rent the DVD. In fact, skip it if you can. But if you have seen it or at least know the plot, you'll remember that the way the devil comes into little Regan, played by Linda Blair, is through a "harmless" Ouija board.

Q: But <u>The Exorcist</u> was just a movie.

A: Of course. But if you talk to priests or ministers who have had experiences with demonic stuff, they say that much of what they saw in that movie was disturbingly accurate, especially the part about the Ouija board. There are a number of good books that talk about this stuff.[5]

Q: What about Wicca? What could be wrong with a religion that honors nature and empowers women?

A: Unfortunately, quite a lot, though few of its practitioners would know it. Perhaps that's what's so frightening. Some people might only want to do good to themselves and others, but they could be unwittingly opening themselves up to forces that mean them great harm. Remember, the dark side always presents itself as other than what it really is. The Bible is emphatic in warning us of this. If Wicca really was what it claimed to be, of course it would be a good thing. But it simply isn't. The fact is that Wicca draws on spiritual power that's not from God. All of the business about honoring nature or women is just PR—and very effective PR at that.

Q: **What about reincarnation? Isn't it possible that we will come back and get a second chance on the God question?**

A: I hate to burst your bubble, but no. At least not if you're interested in what the Bible has to say on the subject.

Q: **Why not?**

A: According to the Bible we are born once and die once and face the judgment seat of God immediately thereafter.[6] There is no second chance. Sorry.

Q: **I have to admit that I was hoping to return as a fly and listen in on secret conversations—to actually be the proverbial fly on the wall...**

A: I hear you, but I'm afraid it's just not going to happen.

Q: **But it seems like getting a second chance would only be fair. What's so terrible about reincarnation?**

A: On the surface, nothing, except for one thing: It's simply not true. Actually there *is* something wrong with it. What's wrong with it is that it can delude people into thinking they'll get a second or third or fourth chance at life on earth, so why decide to follow God now? Why not just put it off? Why should I choose to follow Jesus today when I might get to choose in another lifetime?

   Of course, God wants us to choose immediately because he knows we don't get another chance after this life—and we might not get another chance after today. Any one of us could get hit by a car on the way to the

grocery store, to be perfectly gruesome about it. God
desperately doesn't want to lose us; he loves us and wants
to spend eternity with us. That's what we were created
for. So, obviously, God wants us to choose to follow
him. Putting it off can only lead to no good, and that's
really what the idea of reincarnation seems to lead to,
inevitably.

Q: **Does God influence our lives through the stars?
I've always been curious about this, and I sometimes
read my horoscope.**

A: Well, we have no idea whether the stars have any effect on
our lives, but we do know one thing: God hates astrology
and doesn't want us to dabble in it.

Q: **What?**

A: God forbids astrology. He lumps it in with sorcery and
every kind of demonic, occultic practice. You can read
about it in the Bible.[7] God can be very persnickety and
old-fashioned sometimes, but since he's also infinitely wise
and loving, that's his prerogative.

Q: **What does God have against astrology?**

A: Several things. First of all, like much of what we've been
discussing, astrology is fundamentally occultic. In other
words, there is something ultimately demonic about it.
I know how you hate when I say that... Sorry.

Q: **Come on! About astrology?**

A: I'm not saying that reading the two-line squib next to
Hagar the Horrible or Family Circus is going to make your
head start spinning. But I am saying that according to the
Bible, the source of this knowledge is not God, so by definition it's from the dark side. Go ahead and laugh if you
want, but I'm just telling you what the Bible says on the
subject.

Q: **I'm not laughing.**

A: And even if you don't accept what the Bible says about it,
there are more practical reasons to avoid astrology. In fact,
I'm sure these figure into why God forbids it. For one
thing, it's fatalistic. It tells us that we are this or that, and
we shouldn't marry this one or that one—as if the stars or,
more likely, the astrologists—hold all the cards in our lives.
When the reality is that God holds all the cards. So if you
read the horoscope, and it says, for example, that a Cancer
should never marry a Pisces—and you're a Cancer who is
already married to a Pisces—you would be inclined to think
the stars are suggesting you are in a wrong marriage, and
you'd be better off getting out of it and marrying someone
you are more astrologically compatible with.

Q: **And?**

A: And that is 100 percent contrary to what God would want
you to do. God wants you to honor your marriage vows. He
wants you to let him help you be a better spouse, and he

wants to help your spouse be a better spouse. God can heal a troubled marriage, and he *does* heal troubled marriages. So, yes, astrology is fatalistic. It can be very harmful if you take its advice, which more people do than you realize.

Q: **What if you just read it now and again to get tips on what might be coming up in your life? Or just for fun?**

A: Even then, God forbids it, which is nothing to sneeze at. If God isn't behind it—and he makes it very clear that he isn't—then there is a strong suggestion that a dark spiritual element is involved, one that doesn't wish you well, but that actually wishes to lead you away from the light.

Q: **What does the Bible say about UFOs and aliens?**

A: It says you should avoid them, especially if you've had too much to drink and might say something you'd regret.

Q: **Ha. But seriously, folks...**

A: Seriously, the Bible says absolutely nothing about them, specifically, although I think it's safe to say it still leans heavily in the direction that there isn't any life beyond planet Earth.

Q: **But isn't it arrogant to think that we're the only life in the universe?**

A: Well, first of all, arrogance is an attitude. Someone could be physically attractive and have an arrogant attitude about it, while another person could be just as attractive and have a humble spirit and a good attitude. Many people are attractive or extremely talented or whatever, and some let it go to their heads, while others don't.

So let's say, for argument's sake, that we are the only life in the universe. We could be very arrogant about it, but we could also be humble about it and realize that we didn't put ourselves here, so we shouldn't boast about it. And we didn't create ourselves, so we can't boast about that either. In fact, we have nothing to do with any of it. So the real question isn't whether we are arrogant, but rather whether we really *are* the only life in the universe. That is a question not of attitude but of scientific fact.

And since we can't prove whether we are the *only* life in the universe, we have to make an educated guess based on the best evidence we have.

Q: **What evidence are you referring to?**

A: Actually, there's a lot of it. But before we look at it from a scientific viewpoint, let's briefly look at it from a theological perspective. Let's say that God did create the universe. If that's true, then he could have created it any way he wanted to. He could have created it with life on every planet, or with life on no planets, or with life on one planet—ours. It's his call. So if he did create life just on this one planet, we shouldn't necessarily be surprised. Nor should we be troubled by it, because the assumption is that he knows what he's doing.

And if God loves us so much, which is the main point of the whole Bible, then really, why shouldn't he have gone to the trouble of creating an entire universe with only one planet for people to live on? I mean, as a parent I know I'll go way out of my way for my daughter, all out of proportion to reality, only because I love her so much. If I could give her the sun and the moon and the stars, I would, and most parents are like that. So sometimes I think that God really did create the universe just for us, and that's definitely not because we somehow deserve it, but because he loves us so much that he just wanted to do it for us, even though sometimes we are so far from deserving his love that it breaks his heart.

Q: But what about the scientific evidence?

A: There's a lot of scientific evidence to suggest that the conditions to sustain life in the universe are so staggeringly hard to come by that, statistically speaking, there shouldn't be life on any planets in the universe—*not even one.* And so the fact that there is life on this planet—the fact that Earth meets the insanely impossible criteria for sustaining life—is beyond amazing. It's unbelievable and miraculous, but here we are. This is what is known as the *anthropic principle.* It comes from the Greek word *anthropos,* which means "human," and the anthropic principle suggests that everything on planet Earth is so outrageously fine tuned that it

seems everything was intentionally calibrated so that we
humans could live here.

Q: Okay, what exactly are these finely tuned, life-sustaining elements?

A: For instance, if the Earth were one single percentage point
larger than it is, its gravity would increase just enough to
pull ammonia—which is heavier than oxygen—lower down
into our atmosphere, and we couldn't breathe. If it were just
one single percentage point smaller than it is, its mass
wouldn't have enough gravity to hold oxygen, and it would
evaporate as ammonia does now. So again, we wouldn't be
able to breathe. And if the moon were just one percentage
point bigger than it is now, its gravity would be strong
enough to cause tides measuring hundreds of feet, which
would drown everything in coastal areas and destroy fragile
and necessary coastal ecosystems. But if it were just one percentage point smaller, there wouldn't be enough tide to
cleanse those coastal ecosystems, causing other kinds of
havoc.[8] Of course, those are just a couple of examples.

**Q: So you're saying there is no intelligent life beyond
Earth at all?**

A: It seems there isn't any, but who knows? If God can make
one impossible planet, surely he can make two of them or
two million of them. The Bible does not close the door on
that possibility. As I say, I don't get the impression that
there is life beyond this planet, but if a spaceship suddenly
landed in Times Square, and silver fish-headed beings with

ray guns crawled out of it, I wouldn't lose my faith. I might purchase a firearm and shriek and head for the hills, but I wouldn't lose my faith.

C. S. Lewis wrote a fantastic space trilogy in which he talks about other planets that are populated with all sorts of life forms. In those books—*Out of the Silent Planet, Perelandra,* and *That Hideous Strength*—which I recommend highly, the intelligent creatures are still under the same God we are, but they understand him a bit differently.

So we don't know for sure whether there is life on other planets, but at this point the burden of proof has to be on those who say there is.

When we consider the spiritual realm and things we can't see or explain, we seem to have very little difficulty believing that crystals worn around our necks—or stars that are millions of light-years away—can hold the secrets to our success. But when someone tells us there is a God who created us and loves us and wants us to know him, we tend to cast a wary eye on the whole thing. Is it because when we're talking about a rock or a distant star, everything is impersonal and we can remain at a safe distance? Is it that we are wary of getting involved with Someone who is real and who might ask something of us?

6

Is God Against Us Having a Good Time?

God and Sex; Sex and Marriage; God's View of Pleasure

I can't think of anything that better sums up the way many people feel about religion than this heartbreaking poem by William Blake:

I went to the Garden of Love,
And saw what I never had seen:
A Chapel was built in the midst,
Where I used to play on the green.

And the gates of this Chapel were shut,
And "Thou shalt not" writ over the door;
So I turn'd to the Garden of Love,
That so many sweet flowers bore;

And I saw it was filled with graves,
And tombstones where flowers should be;
And Priests in black gowns were walking their rounds,
And binding with briers my joys and desires.[1]

The only God most people have ever heard about seems to be the one who is a dour, grim-faced moral policeman—a cosmic kill-joy. How did that ever happen?

Q: Okay, what does God think about sex?

A: Generally speaking, he thinks it's one of the greatest things in existence. Probably because he invented it and because it's the way humans reproduce, which he has specifically told us to do.

Q: Then why do so many people make it sound as if God is against sex?

A: God isn't against sex at all. Quite the contrary. But perhaps because he thinks so highly of it, he has very high standards for how it should be used—and how it should *not* be used.

Q: Like for pleasure? We're only supposed to have sex to procreate, is that it?

A: Not at all! But when we use it *only* for our pleasure—which is to say, in a completely selfish way—we are missing out on the core of what God made sex for, and in a sense, by definition, we are missing it—twisting it all out of shape, really. Think of it this way: Sex is an extraordinary gift God has given us, but he wants it to be used in a way that is appropriate, that acknowledges its extraordinary value, and that acknowledges the gift giver. Why is that so terrible?

Q: I could use some clarification on that last point.

A: Okay, imagine if a mom and dad give their ten-year-old son
a bicycle. It's a very expensive bicycle, and they've gone to
considerable trouble to pick it out. They can't wait to see
the look of joy on their son's face when they give it to him.
They know he'll love it and get years of pleasure out of it.
He will get exercise and plenty of fresh air. And he will now
have a way to enjoy all sorts of things he couldn't enjoy
when he was stuck on his block with no way to get around.

But then imagine that when they give the boy the bicycle, he takes it and splits, without so much as a thank-you.
He takes the bike, uses it in a way that trashes it completely,
and he destroys it in a few weeks. The parents are upset
because their son was supposed to enjoy this bicycle for
years—but because he didn't care about his parents' wishes,
he lost out on the great things they intended for him.

Q: Okay...

A: Well, that's what it's like when we take this outrageously
wonderful gift called sex and use it in a way that's contrary
to what God intended.

Q: Like how?

A: Again, using sex without a thought to its true value, solely
as a means of self-gratification. It's taking something extra-
ordinarily multifaceted and using it for a single, dull pur-
pose. It's something like using a laptop computer to
hammer nails.

Q: Okay, if sex isn't for personal gratification, then what exactly is it for?

A: Consider this: God has made a way for two human beings to be united in a mutually ecstatic way, and out of this ecstasy comes the miracle of miracles, life. But wait, there's more! God created us male and female so that the sexual act is a picture of his relationship with those who follow him.

I'm going to get graphic for a moment, so you might want to send the kids out of the room. In this picture the followers of Jesus are cast in the role of the bride, and God is cast in the role of the bridegroom. And the sex is seen as utterly and entirely positive. Those who believe in God yield to him—freely—and by yielding to him, they experience ecstasy. And life comes out of this union. Life! Basically, when a person yields to God, the result is ecstasy and life. And life, of course, continues to grow and grow and yield more life.

The sexual act is also a picture of how the union between two people is sealed. I might say I love someone, but in marriage and the consummation of the marriage through sex, I am saying that I commit myself fully, with nothing held back. This love is not just a feeling; it's a blood oath. I'm saying that I belong to my spouse, freely, and she is saying she belongs to me. The stakes are huge. We are making

> Using sex just for self-gratification is like
> using a laptop computer to hammer nails.

a lifelong covenant with each other, of our own free will. It's an incredibly romantic and beautiful thing. And the sexual act is the final consummation of that extraordinary covenant.

So you can see how God might be bummed out if we take this extraordinary gift and use it stupidly or selfishly.

Q: **You're talking about sex being limited to marriage. But what about the idea that marriage is just a piece of paper?**

A: Well, if you put a Rembrandt in the bottom of a birdcage, you are using it as though it *were* a piece of paper. But it's not just a piece of paper; it's a sublime work of art. Marriage isn't just a piece of paper either. It's a masterpiece and a mystery, and it not only connects two people to each other in a sacred way; it also connects those two people to God in a way they hadn't been connected to him before.

People are entitled to think what they want. But if you want to know what God thinks of marriage—and he's the one who invented it—you'll see that he created it to be a picture and image of his covenant with the people he created. He is utterly committed to us. He makes extreme sacrifices for us. And his commitment is not based on a feeling. Even if we hurt him or turn away from him, he tries to woo us back and never abandons us. That's how he sees marriage, and that's what he created sex for.

Q: But isn't God vaguely against pleasure in general?

A: Not even slightly. As with sex, God created all pleasure specifically for us. It's when we seek pleasure outside his will that we mess things up.

Q: So if I were to decide to believe in God, it doesn't mean I'd have to give up pleasure?

A: Not at all. The idea that God is against pleasure couldn't be more wrong. Everything that's good comes from God—everything.

Q: Then where does the idea come from that God is against pleasure?

A: From any number of places. People have this completely wrongheaded idea that being "spiritual" means forgoing all pleasure. Most Eastern religions teach this, and many confused Christians over the years have taught it and attempted to live it. But it's nowhere to be found in the Bible. It's not God's plan. Usually ascetics (people who deny themselves pleasure) have this idea that they can earn their way into heaven by what they do—or don't do.

Q: Then all asceticism is wrong?

A: Not at all. Just like pleasure, asceticism has its role in our lives, and if we use it to bring us closer to God, as many people have, it can be an extraordinary thing. Many monks, especially, have used fasting from any number of things as a way to focus more completely on God. It's a tricky balance, though, between getting closer to God through asceticism and trying to impress him by asceticism. Or, in some cases, trying to manipulate him into giving us what we want because we've been denying ourselves certain things.

This goes back to the candy-machine idea of God. I press this button and expect certain results. I do this, so God must do that. Or I avoid doing this, so now God must do something for me. God isn't a machine to be manipulated, with buttons that we press. He is a someone who loves us and wants a relationship with us that will be endlessly gratifying and fulfilling—which is so much more than having a God who simply grants or denies what we want based on what we do or don't do. God is not that sort of a God. He desperately wants us to know him as he really is, as the loving Father who wants to bless us in ways we can hardly imagine.

Q: God actually <u>wants</u> us to have pleasure?

A: Absolutely. He's our heavenly Parent, and all parents want their kids to experience pleasure. But parents know that indulging in too much pleasure in the wrong ways will lead to pain and suffering. Imagine a kid who loves cotton candy. Naturally, the parent wants to give the kid cotton candy once in a while. But what if the kid wants cotton candy every day? What if she wants it instead of all other food? Of course the parent wants to please the child; the parent loves the child wholeheartedly. But the parent knows that if the child gets her way, she'll get sick. Too much cotton candy will lead to poor health and certainly to a very, very bad case of tooth decay. Is that what a loving parent wants?

Q: Obviously not.

A: So the parent has to say no, has to *deny* the child pleasure. But that's only because the parent wants the child to have more pleasure in the long term. Similarly, God wants us to have as much pleasure and joy as possible, but he knows that because of the way we are made, we will enjoy life more in every way if we abide by certain restrictions. The restrictions will make life *more* fun and *more* pleasurable.

Jesus said, "I have come that they may have life, and that they may have it more abundantly."[2] Children are full of life and joy and hope, and Jesus loves them. In fact, he said that in order to enter the kingdom of God, we have to become like children. There is nothing dour about a God like that.

7

Does God Hate Gays and Oppose Women?

Hateful Christians; God and Gays; God's View of Women

In the spring of 1945, a thirty-nine-year-old Lutheran pastor was hanged in the Flossenberg Concentration Camp, just days before its liberation by the Allies. Dietrich Bonhoeffer's deep Christian faith would not allow him to stand by while the inhuman influence of Naziism spread throughout his beloved Germany. In the 1930s he and other pastors in what was called the Confessing Church stood up to Hitler, speaking out boldly against the Third Reich's treatment of the Jews and excoriating other German Christians for their shameful lack of courage in confronting the evil among them. In 1939 Bonhoeffer traveled to New York City to teach at Union Theological Seminary, but his conscience did not let him stay. He returned to his homeland where, during the war, he aided the resistance and helped smuggle many Jews out of the country. Finally, reversing his earlier pacifism, he got involved in a plot to kill Hitler, for which the Gestapo eventually imprisoned and executed him. The God of the Bible calls people of faith to stand up against the persecution of the powerless, even at the cost of their own lives.

Q: Christians seem to go out of their way to point out that the Bible condemns homosexuality. Does God actually hate gays as some of them say he does?

A: The Bible is magnificently consistent on this one thing: God loves all people, no matter what. We are created in God's image, and there is nothing we can do to make him love any one of us any less. This doesn't mean he loves everything we do. Anything that hurts us he is strongly *against.* In fact, that's what the Bible calls "sin."

So when you wonder whether God hates gays, the answer is an emphatic *no.* God loves every one of us, period, case closed. God loves us all, even and perhaps especially when we stray from his plan for us, whether brazenly or simply out of confusion or as a misguided way of dealing with our pain. If people of faith see themselves as sinners in need of God's direction and help—which is what the Bible teaches—it becomes impossible not to love others who are struggling just as we are, although perhaps differently. People who know God also love other people because God loves them and because he will never give up on them.

Q: Sounds pretty condescending to me.

A: Yes, that's a problem, isn't it? But how can a human ever perfectly express what God wants from us? We always mess it up somehow. But we have to try, don't we? We can't *not* try to lovingly represent God just because we know we'll do it imperfectly. The bottom line is that those who follow God have to have genuine love and compassion for others, and if we recognize how profoundly messed up we ourselves are, we will have compassion for other people. So if people don't have serious humility about their own state of affairs, they should probably keep their mouths shut. God doesn't want his followers to add to the pain of the people he loves. He wants his children to treat others as people he desperately loves.

> God loves every one of us, period, case closed.

Q: **What about that guy who keeps showing up in the news with the signs that say "God hates fags"?**

A: Not to judge, but I think he has some major issues.

Q: **But he has a real knack for getting on television, you have to admit.**

A: True. It's pretty impressive. But that's not what we were talking about. All I can say about people like that is "God help anyone who condemns those whom God loves." But even my hostility toward those who are judgmental isn't right. I'm supposed to love my enemies. So you start out furious at the guy who goes around with the hateful signs, but in the end you hope to see even him as God does, as another one of those confused people to whom God longs to reach out.

You know that when God sees us hurting each other, it breaks his heart. If we could see God's love for us—for every single person—we would all be radically changed.

Q: This is very different from what I've heard other Christians say. What about the idea that God is angry at sin?

A: Of course he's angry at sin. But it's mainly the sin, not the sinners, that gets him angry. Even if we want to see him as angry at us, he's only angry at us temporarily—and because he loves us, certainly not because he hates us. God hates the sin we commit because he hates anything that hurts us, and he will do anything to warn us against it. But he can't force us to choose against sin, as we talked about earlier.

God knows far better than we ever can that our actions have consequences and that many times we hurt ourselves by the things we choose to do. If we do certain things, we will end up suffering for it. God gives us rules and commandments to prevent us from hurting ourselves and others—to increase our joy, not to kill it. So if you're harming yourself, God will scream at you, in a way, because you are harming someone who is infinitely precious to him—yourself! He does this because he loves you, not because he hates you. He loves all of us passionately, more deeply than we can really ever grasp.

Q: But isn't the Bible undeniably anti-woman? And doesn't that mean God is therefore anti-woman?

A: The short answer to this one is that the Bible is definitely and emphatically *not* anti-woman. In fact, it's just the opposite. Ditto for God.

Q: How is God not anti-woman?

A: Well, he's not pro-woman and anti-man or anti-woman and pro-man. He's pro-woman and pro-man. He loves men and women equally.

God created men and women in his image. In Genesis it says, "Male and female He created them."[1] It's clear that, together, men and women are made in his image. And we are unique in this. Nothing else in creation is made in God's image. Which means that both men and women are accorded extraordinary and unique status. We both bear the *imago dei,* the image of God, in our persons, equally. Any person cannot be anything other than a glorious creature whom God adores, because we all bear his image.

Q: But let's be honest. From the Bible you get the idea that women are second-class citizens.

A: The cultures depicted in the Bible were backwards in any number of ways, yes. But that doesn't mean God approved of those cultures. The Bible was written in societies where slavery was the norm, for example, but the Bible certainly doesn't promote slavery.

And as far as women go, Jesus was radically ahead of his time in his attitude toward them. There are numerous examples in the Bible of how his behavior toward women flew in the face of conventional views and customs. There's that famous scene where Jesus was talking to a Samaritan woman at a well. It would have been scandalous for a man to be seen talking with a woman, especially since they were alone. And even more outrageous, a Jew talking to a

Samaritan! But that's what Jesus did. And you don't hear it much, but two of his very closest friends were women: Mary and Martha, Lazarus's sisters. And the first people to see Jesus after the resurrection were women.[2] I could go on, but you get the idea.

History often glosses over the profoundly pagan underpinnings of the Third Reich, which persecuted and murdered six million Jews, demonized homosexuals, and saw women as little more than breeding machines for the Reich. Hitler's secular "survival of the fittest" Social Darwinism stands in stark contrast to the philosophy of both the Old and New Testaments, which preach the inherent dignity and immutable sanctity of every single human being. God seeks justice for the powerless and the marginalized.

8

Why Does Anyone Need Religion?

Ritual and Superstition; God's Stance on Religion

I n 1969 Woody Allen had an hour-long television special on ABC. It featured what you'd expect—some classic stand-up shtick and a couple of skits. But toward the middle of the hour, it included something so strange I will never forget it. Two chairs were set on the stage, and for ten minutes Woody Allen had a conversation with someone you wouldn't have expected to see him talking with on a TV special. The man was Billy Graham.

What possessed Woody Allen to have a conversation with the most famous evangelist of the twentieth century on national television in front of millions of people? Did he see something authentic in the man, something that, for all its foreignness, he couldn't discount? Did he see more than someone who holds certain beliefs and who spends his life trying to convince others that he's right about those beliefs? Perhaps he saw something that transcended mere religion, something that spoke of truth itself.

Q: Isn't it true that some people are just religious and others aren't? Why do I have to be religious if that's not who I am?

A: Well, this brings up the whole subject of what it means to be religious. So in order to answer your question, I have to address that first. Having a relationship with God is not the same as being religious. Many people are religious and have zero relationship with God. In fact, being religious can be a bad thing.

Q: I'm surprised to hear you say that.

A: It really can. The fact is that religion can be a way of hiding from God, of trying to fool him.

Q: You're losing me.

A: Think about it. Some people think that by going to church or synagogue, or by reading the scriptures regularly, or by following other rituals, or by *not* doing certain things, they are somehow good enough to warrant going to heaven.

Q: What's wrong with that? It sounds as if they're doing exactly what God wants them to be doing.

A: On one level, yes. But on another level they are trying to fool God with their actions. And they are totally cutting God out of the picture by saying that if they do X and Y and Z, they automatically *earn* heaven, as if it were a system of rules, and they could simply play the game and win. The idea of a moral structure that cuts God out of the picture is very attractive to humans because that puts *us* in control. But God wants us to understand that without a relationship with him, moral behavior isn't worth anything. Mere moral rectitude doesn't fool God. The Pharisees of the first century were morally upright, but Jesus blasted them for being hypocrites.[1] The fact is that God is offended by people who do everything right and think it somehow earns them gold stars and an automatic free pass into heaven.

Q: God is offended when we do good things? That seems totally impossible.

A: You have much to learn, grasshopper. Seriously, think about it. The Bible says that God looks at our hearts. So if you're doing good things but from a wrong motive, God sees the inward *motive,* not the good things you're doing. He isn't fooled. Many people are doing things that outwardly everyone sees as "good," but the only reason they are doing those things is for a bad reason. Shocking, but true.

Q: What's a bad reason to do something good?

A: One bad reason might be merely to get praise from other people. Or to feel like a big shot—or to feel that you're better than other people who aren't doing as many good things as you are. Or sometimes, people will do good things just to get God off their backs.

Q: **That I don't get.**

A: You know, like a kid doing a chore just to get his parents to let him do something he wants to do, or so he can get something special from them. It's a kind of manipulation. Perhaps inwardly he hates his parents but figures "if I play the game and take out the trash, they'll let me go out with my friends and do as I please." His heart is in the wrong place. Some folks refuse to give God their hearts, but they figure they don't need to, because they believe it's all about performance. So when they do certain good things, they figure God owes them something.

Q: **What do they think God owes them?**

A: Any number of things. A good life, a prosperous life, a happy life without pain or tragedy. Entrance to heaven...

Q: **So?**

A: So God doesn't owe us anything. He is our loving Father who would do anything for us; he's not some adversary we are bargaining with! He wants us to see that, and to see that if he gives us good things, it's because he loves us, not because he owes us. Big difference. How offended would any father or mother be if their children avoided them and did only what they thought could get their parents to give them an inheritance?

Q: **I suppose they'd be pretty offended.**

A: Parents want three things from their children more than anything else in life. They want their children's love, attention, and time. If they have that type of relationship with their children, all kinds of other good stuff comes out of it, and generally the children will want to please their parents. But sometimes children try to manipulate their parents just so they can get something in return. Parents want an honest and authentic relationship, not manipulation. If they have a real relationship, then even when the children fail, the parents still love and forgive them. But a child who deceives his parent cuts that parent out of any real relationship.

For many people, being religious and morally "good" are nothing more than fancy ways of trying to manipulate God into giving them what they want. It's just like Adam and Eve in the Garden of Eden, when they put on fig leaves to hide their nakedness from God. As if!

Q: I forgot about that.

A: They actually thought they could fool God, the Almighty, who knows *everything*. What a sad joke, really.

Q: So God doesn't want us to be religious. He wants us to have a relationship with him?

A: I guess it sounds a little pathetic if you put it that way. But think of it this way: Is it pathetic that your parents want a relationship with you?

Q: No, but they're not God.

A: That logic holds only if God is some aloof, distant deity, and not the loving Father described in the Bible. Jesus himself referred to God as "Father." In fact, he used the

Aramaic word *Abba*—which is closer to "Daddy" or "Papa"—which gives us an apt picture of the great intimacy they had with each other. Someone we call "Father" might still be distant and aloof and even frightening, but how can a Papa be that? That's how Jesus referred to his Father, and he told us to do the same. I, for one, am glad he did.

Q: When did he tell us to call God "Daddy"?

A: When he gave us what is called the Lord's Prayer. Jesus' closest followers had asked him to teach them how to pray. And the Lord's Prayer was his answer. The first words of the prayer are "Our Father." But again, the real word Jesus used was *Abba* or "Daddy." So he was telling them (and us) to pray to their (and our) heavenly "Papa"—the intimate Father who loved them and cherished them—not some aloof deity who wanted them to perform moral feats on which he would judge them.

Q: Isn't characterizing God as "Daddy" a bit disrespectful?

A: That's the other side of the coin. While God is our loving and intimate "Papa," he is also the infinitely powerful and all-knowing Creator of the universe. Sometimes people go too far in the direction of thinking of him as their pal, and they forget that he is the one who, in a single moment, spoke billions of vast galaxies into being *out of nothing* and who this moment sustains the entire universe and everything in it, including, and perhaps especially, us.

Q: So how do you reconcile seeing God as "Daddy" with
this awesome "Ruler of the universe" idea?

A: It's right there in the Lord's Prayer. The first line is "Our
Father [Abba] in heaven, hallowed be Your name."[2] We are
talking to our cherished and loving "Papa," but Jesus said
his name should be "hallowed"—which is another word for
"holy" or "made holy" or "sacred." God is incredibly familiar and incredibly awesome at the same time.

Q: Okay, while you're on the subject, what exactly does
"holy" mean?

A: It means "set apart," in the sense that something is set apart
when it is sacred. And of course that means that whatever is
holy or sacred is set apart from all that is *not* holy or sacred.

So in the Lord's Prayer, Jesus was saying that God's
name is sacred, and we should remember that at all times,
just as we should remember God's love for us at all times.
Somehow we have to hold these two extremely disparate
things together—the idea that God is our loving Father
who wants us to climb up on his lap so he can hold us
and hug us and enjoy us the way a parent enjoys spending
time with a little child, and the very different idea that this
loving Father is the King of kings whose slightest word can
create galaxies beyond numbering.

But if you think about it, this juxtaposition of two infinitely different things is exactly what makes knowing God
so glorious. Our "Daddy" is the King of the universe. It's
like having a dad who is president, only multiplied by

about a billion. We've all seen those old *Life* magazine photos of two-year-old John-John Kennedy crawling around the floor of the Oval Office. It's the same with God, only much more so. Just as a president will allow his child to crawl into the Oval Office and take liberties that no one else would ever be allowed, so God—who has the right and the ability to make us tremble with fear—instead, lovingly welcomes us in. This is an extraordinary thing, well worth mulling over.

Q: Can we get back your statement about how religion can be a bad thing?

A: Yes, well, religion in the negative sense of simply being a bunch of rules and rituals is pretty much the same as superstition. Without a relationship with God at its core, all religion devolves to superstition. And superstition—whether or not a person calls it that—is against what God wants for us. Or to use an old-fashioned word, it's an abomination. What a word: *abomination!* Anyway, that's what superstition is to God.

Q: And why is that?

A: Because, again, superstition is a way of trying to manipulate God. If I wear this rabbit's foot or medal, or even if I cross myself robotically, just going through the motions, I am in essence trying to "magically" force God to do good things for me. But what's really behind my superstition is fear.

There's no love or joy or peace in that sort of thing, only fear. God doesn't want us to be afraid of him in that sense, to think he's really just looking for a good excuse to whack us. Too many religious people live in fear—"If I don't cross myself this way and if I don't wear this amulet and if I don't go through this ritual, I'm done for!" That's all fear. God has nothing to do with that, and one of the most harmful things in human history is when people have confused fear-based superstition with faith in God.

> Without a relationship with God at its core,
> all religion devolves to superstition.

Q: So I can be confident that God doesn't want to whack me?

A: You can take it to the bank. He is our loving Father, and he is looking for ways to help us, to save us from trouble, not to trip us up or punish us.

God is on our side. He's the *Captain* of our side, the beloved Coach. If we see him for who he really is, we'll want to play our hearts out for him because we love him, not because we fear his punishment if we fail.

Q: God as Gipper, eh?

A: Actually, yes, on some level that's dead on, but don't quote me on it.

Q: Isn't religion just divisive? And haven't more people been killed in the name of religion than for any other reason?

A: Well, of course religion can be divisive. So can sports. What about it? And no, more people *haven't* been killed in the name of religion than for any other reason. In fact it's precisely the opposite. Still, it's a very widespread misperception. You hear it all the time.

Q: Would you care to elaborate?

A: Okay. First of all, if only *one* person had been killed in the name of religion, that would be one person too many. The idea of it is horrible. Let's get that out of the way right off the bat.

But if we are talking facts and figures, the precise opposite of what most people believe on this subject is actually true. History tells us that in all of the inquisitions and crusades, approximately three thousand people were killed, total. And that is over the course of several centuries. Again, one person killed is far too many, but you'd think the number would be infinitely larger than three thousand over the centuries, based on what you generally hear.

But here's where things get extremely interesting. Look at the comparison with what happened under various political regimes guided by secular and militantly atheistic ideologies. Atheistic regimes such as Stalin's, Hitler's, Pol Pot's, and Mao's murdered 100 *million* people in the twentieth century alone. That's a ratio of about 300,000 people killed by atheistic regimes for every one person killed in the name of Christianity. Kind of puts things in perspective, doesn't it? So from the point of view of history and statistics, by far the most dangerous ideologies on the planet—by a chilling ratio of about 300,000 to 1—are secular and atheistic ideologies. It really is frightening. And you can also say that just because someone was killed in the "name" of religion doesn't mean that the people doing the killing were doing God's will. On the contrary, they were working *against* God's will. It's like pacifists killing people in the name of pacifism. It makes no sense.

Some people are religious, and some aren't, but everyone is searching for the truth. Most people who are searching for truth have a sense of what it might look like if they stumbled across it. It's something that is real, that touches the human soul, that answers the questions our minds haven't even formed yet but that our hearts long to have answered.

Religion can come across as boring; worse than that, it can come across as phony. Proponents of mere religion can come across as boring and phony too. But the truth isn't like that. It might not be what we want it to be. Aspects of it might make us uncomfortable. But the truth is never boring. And it's certainly never phony. If and when we find it, it might even be a bit frightening at first, but it will always be compelling and powerful and beautiful.

9

Isn't One Religion About as Good as Another?

*How Religions Compare; Allah and God;
The Meaning of Mercy*

As everyone in today's world knows, tolerance is important. If I say blue is the best color and you say red is the best color, we have different points of view. And since favorite colors are fundamentally personal and subjective, neither of us is really right or wrong. So we agree to disagree; we tolerate each other's opinions.

But what happens when we're dealing with objective truth, like one plus one equals two? The statement "one plus one equals two" can't have the same validity as the statement "one plus one equals three." To be intellectually honest, I'm forced to choose one or the other. There's no way out. Both statements can't be true.

Does this mean I'm being intolerant of the person who believes that one and one make three?

Q: Don't all religions really worship the same God?

A: Well, yes and no. First of all, *yes,* because there *is* only one God. It's not as if he has three or four siblings to choose from, depending on our personal preferences. There is just one God, and there has always been only one God.

God created the universe *ex nihilo*—out of nothing—and he invented atomic and subatomic structures and spiders and Noam Chomsky and Charo, among other things. Everything that exists, he invented. There simply *is* no other God, and we are stuck with him, no matter what religion we claim to belong to—or *refuse* to claim to belong to.

Q: Okay...

A: So, on the one hand, *yes.* And on the other hand, *no,* all religions *don't* worship the same God. Because even though there is only one God, some religions have a distorted view of who he is, which confuses things. They worship a version of God that is not exactly the God of the Bible.

Q: You're losing me.

A: This is always tough to explain.

Q: Please try.

A: Okay, this might sound weird, but imagine that I was a member of a President George Washington fan club, but I firmly believed that George was a startlingly obese guy who had lived in Vermont.

Q: **Say what?**

A: Think about it. We know there is only one President George Washington. But imagine that somehow I insisted that that George Washington—who was born in 1732 and became the first president of the United States—was *also* a seriously tubby guy who lived in ski country his whole life. It makes no sense, and yet imagine that that's who I think George Washington was. Just because I seem to be talking about George Washington doesn't necessarily mean I have any real or accurate idea of what George Washington was like. Perhaps I'm overstating the case.

Q: **Perhaps.**

A: All I'm saying is that God is who God is, and we can't go around believing whatever we want to believe about him any more than people can believe what they want to believe about George Washington. Facts are facts, and we're bound by them. And some religions have gotten some of the facts about God a little bit confused, and so their theology is a little off center—if you're talking about the God of the Bible.

Q: **And?**

A: And it's no different than someone who gets the biographical facts of Washington a little messed up and erroneously believes that he was a balloon-shaped gentleman from the Green Mountain State. Not that there'd be anything wrong with such a man, but he just wasn't our first president.

Q: Okay...

A: At the same time, someone could be a member of a religion that has an unbiblical idea of who God is, but in her *heart* that particular person might be praying to God as God really is. The person might fully intend to worship the real God but has a few details wrong. Someone might belong to a religion that has an off-center theology, but that person simply might be ignorant of that theology and therefore untainted by it. In her heart, the person might be praying to God as God *really* is. God looks at our hearts more than he looks at the belief statements of the people we associate with. Not that theological beliefs aren't important. They are hugely important. But what's in an individual's heart is far more important to God.

Q: So where are you going with all of this?

A: I'm just saying that someone could belong to a religion that claims to worship Athena or Baal or Ashtaroth or Donald Duck, and yet that person in her private prayers might be talking to the actual God of the universe, who is all-loving and all-merciful. And God will hear that prayer.[1]

Q: I have to admit I wasn't expecting this, but I think I know what you're saying.

A: We might worship God in the same building as people who have some very wrongheaded ideas about God. But if in our hearts we are praying to God—to the actual God—to the extent that he has been revealed to us at that point, he hears our prayers. He can hear what we *mean* because he cuts through the static amazingly well. He knows what we *really* mean, deep in our hearts, better even than we do.

Q: **Is there anything else?**

A: Yes, there's one other thing about God and religion: Some religions don't believe in any God at all. Some religions are atheistic.

Q: **Some religions don't believe in God?**

A: Correct.

> Some religions don't believe in any God at all.
> Some religions are atheistic.

Q: **I find that genuinely impossible to believe.**

A: From our point of view it makes absolutely no sense. But it's a fact. For example, Hinduism is an atheistic religion.

Q: **Okay, I'll ask the obvious: How can a religion be atheistic? I thought religion was all about God.**

A: You'd think so, wouldn't you? But Hinduism is basically an ethical system that doesn't include a belief in any kind of Creator God the way Jews, Muslims, and Christians do. We assume that all religions have to do with some sort of supreme, almighty being, but Hinduism doesn't.

Q: **Amazing.**

A: Hey, can I ask you a question?

Q: I suppose.

A: Okay. What do you say to a Hindu hot-dog vendor?

Q: I don't know. What <u>do</u> you say to a Hindu hot-dog vendor?

A: Make me one with everything.

Q: Ha.

Q: Is the God of Islam, Allah, the same as the God described in the Bible?

A: That's a really tricky question. Some would say "yes," and some would say "yes, but," and still others would say "no." Of course the smartest people would duck the whole question entirely.

Q: So what do <u>you</u> say?

A: I'd begin by saying that many Muslims would say *no,* God and Allah are not the same. According to most serious Muslims, the idea that a Christian or Jew believes in the same God they do is simply impossible, no matter how much Americans would like to believe it. Americans also assume that everyone on the planet is addicted to ketchup. It's a charming way we have of projecting our own frame of reference on everyone else, in a well-meaning sort of way, of course. So it might sound a bit harsh to us, but according to Islam, Christians and Jews are, well, you've heard the term *infidels*. Some of us may be very nice infidels, but we aren't going to impress any serious Muslims with our particular faith claims.

Q: This sounds a bit severe.

A: Perhaps, but it's what the Koran teaches, and even if we don't agree with it, we can't make it say what we want it to say. We have to take it at face value, however uncomfortable that may be. Many Muslim people might not think this, but most serious Muslim theologians would, and we have to see it from their point of view. You have to respect someone's beliefs enough to at least see them for what they are.

Q: So, how is Allah different from the God of the Bible?

A: Again, we don't know what's in a person's heart. So a Muslim might be praying to the God of the Bible, and many do just that. But the theology of the Koran is a different thing, and that's what we're talking about. To be totally simplistic about it, Islam officially believes in a God who is very into right and wrong in a black-and-white way, rather than in a God of forgiveness and love. Of course, some people have a so-called Christian faith that is just as lacking in mercy. We've all met them. But I would argue that's not a *real* Christian faith, because a real Christian faith understands the concept of *grace*. Certainly that's what Christian theology is all about, even if some Christians don't get it or practice it. Grace is inescapably at the heart of the Christian faith. Without grace Christians are just clucking moralists—or moralistic clucks—and they can be very annoying because they are usually telling you that they are more moral than you are. That's the sort of thing that leads to persecution and bigotry and religious pride and hypocrisy. Grace, on the other hand, leads to humility, because a truly humble person knows he is inherently no better than the worst person on the planet.

Q: But how is it that Christians have a monopoly on grace?

A: Christians don't have a monopoly on grace by any stretch of the imagination. *God* has a monopoly on grace. But despite Christians' often graceless behavior, Christian theology is the only theology that puts God's grace at the center of everything.

Q: How is Christianity unique in that regard?

A: By means of the central event of the Christian faith: Jesus' death on the cross. The idea is that Jesus' death is the only thing that makes it possible for us to enter heaven. He paid the price for our sins. It's his grace toward us, demonstrated in that act, that allows us to be close to God, to have a relationship with God, and to go to heaven. It's based on what Jesus did for us out of love for us, not on anything we do. So it's all about his grace, not about our moral performance. Of course, human beings are so prone to pride that, ironically, Christians will sometimes be prideful about the idea that grace is at the center of Christianity, as if to say, "We have the best religion!"

But if you can see past the problem of religious pride, you'll see that grace is an extraordinary and infinitely wonderful thing. And it's available to everyone, certainly not just Christians. What makes it available is Jesus and his voluntary death on the cross. But because grace is at the core of Christian theology, Christians sometimes act as if they invented it, which they didn't. God did.

Q: I'm still not clear on the connection between Jesus' crucifixion and the idea of grace.

A: Well, Jesus' death on the cross is the ultimate illustration of God's grace toward us. According to Christian teaching, Jesus died in our place. His willingness to do that shows his love for us—it shows us God's grace. So those of us who aren't totally up to snuff morally—which would be *every one* of us—need not be judged for our failings. Instead, we can be forgiven by God through accepting his grace to us in Jesus' sacrifice.

Q: And Islam doesn't teach anything like this?

A: No, Islam basically says you *will* be judged by your behavior, so you'd better behave!

Q: Oh, behave!

A: Exactly. Of course, many Christians are not any different in their thinking. They think it's about what they do or don't do, and that you have to behave in the right way to get into heaven. But they are missing the entire point of their own faith. It's all so ironic.

Q: Doesn't Islam believe in Jesus at all?

A: Yes—and no. It's tremendously confusing because Islam
    says that Jesus is not God and is not the Messiah. It teaches
    that he was only a prophet, and not even as great a prophet
    as Muhammad. But more important, it teaches that Jesus'
    resurrection was a sham and a hoax. Now, forgive me, but if
    you don't get the part about Jesus' death and resurrection,
    you are missing the fundamental point of who he was.

    Christians believe that God is a God of love and for-
    giveness more than anything else. And the cross is at the
    heart of this. So Jesus' perfect life and his voluntary death
    on the cross and subsequent resurrection make it possible
    for us to get to heaven. God says that Jesus will trade us his
    perfection for our imperfection because he loves us. We
    don't need to be morally perfect, nor can we be. But Jesus
    was. So God says that if we accept the free gift of his grace,
    we are effectively treated as though we were morally perfect
    and perfectly righteous. Just as Jesus was. We are welcomed
    in as God's sons and daughters. Which is absolutely amaz-
    ing if you stop and think about it.

Q: But that's Christianity, just one of hundreds of
    religions. A lot of bright, knowledgeable people
    would disagree with the idea that Christianity is
    fundamentally different from any other religious
    system.

A: Of course, they would. And most of them would mean
    well, but both sides can't be right on this question. We have
    to be logical. Either Jesus was God and died on the cross

and then rose bodily from the dead, thereby destroying sin and death and making it possible for us to be with him in paradise forever, or having faith in him is bogus. Period. Without the central events of Jesus' crucifixion and resurrection, you simply don't have Christianity. You can call it Christianity, but it's not. All religions are not alike, so ultimately you have to choose.

One reason that talking about religion gets confusing is that a lot of people confuse God with religion. Religion is important, and it's well worth investigating. But God is separate from religion, and God's nature and character transcend religion.

The best religion directs people to God, helping to clarify who God is and what he seeks from us. The worst religion calls attention to itself and glorifies human thought and tradition, obscuring our view of God. So religion can be either good or bad, while God is always and unconditionally good.

All truth claims can't be equal. If someone says Jesus is God and someone else says he's not, both can't be right. You can respect and tolerate people on both sides of the controversy, but you can't *be* on both sides. One way or the other, you have to choose.

10

What's the *Real* Story on Adam and Eve?

*Forbidden Fruit; Falling from Grace;
Made in God's Image*

The shortest poem in the entire English language is "Fleas" and is widely attributed to Ogden Nash. In this three-word poem, Adam is said to be infested with the tiny critters.

I admit having been tempted to try and write a shorter poem—and failing. But I can lay claim to having written a poem that might be the second shortest in the English language. My runner-up poem is obviously inspired by "Fleas." It's titled "Bellybuttons," and the poem, in its entirety, is: "Eve and Adam / Never had 'em." Of course, we can't know for sure that they didn't, but it makes the point that they were the only two humans not born from a womb, and therefore, they probably wouldn't have had umbilical cords or navels. But who can say for sure? On some things the Bible is eerily silent. That is one of them.

Q: Did Adam and Eve actually exist?

A: You're big on this whole existence thing, aren't you?

Q: I like things to exist if I'm going to be taking them seriously.

A: Well, yes, Adam and Eve did exist. Some people would say they existed mythologically, but not literally. I have no idea what that means, so I'll assume they existed literally, although it's impossible to know exactly *when* they existed. All of their birth records were destroyed in Noah's flood.

Q: You're kidding.

A: Of course I'm kidding. That was a joke. But seriously, Jesus spoke of them as existing, and he wasn't given to hyperbole on important theological matters.

Q: Do you believe Adam and Eve actually ate an apple, messing things up for the rest of humanity when they decided to disobey God?

A: Yes. But it wasn't an apple. It was some kind of forbidden fruit, but not necessarily an apple.

Q: No way!

A: Way! Look it up. But who cares what kind of fruit it was. Maybe it was a tangelo or an ugly fruit or whatever. Actually, it couldn't have been an ugly fruit because the Bible says it was "pleasing to the eye."[1] Anyway, the point is that there was an actual tree and an actual piece of fruit and two actual human beings. It may have happened outside of

time, in an eternal "time before time" as we know it. Hard
to say for sure. It seems that time as we know it began
when Adam and Eve fell from grace after eating the fruit.
Before that they were in a kind of endless present, an eternity just like the eternity that awaits us after this earthly life.

Q: **It's sort of hard to accept the idea of an eternity
before time.**

A: Yes, it is. But it's not one of those things that's a deal
breaker as far as faith is concerned. God isn't going to quiz
us on this sort of thing. And even scientists routinely talk
about time as being something that only began existing
when the universe began, like about 18 billion years ago.
Time is not a constant or a given. Even Einstein knew that.

Q: **Let's get back to the idea of falling from grace. So
Adam and Eve ate an apple—excuse me, a piece of
forbidden fruit. What's the big problem with that?**

A: The idea of the Fall, as it's called in Christian theology, is
really compelling. Think of it. Adam and Eve are the apples
of God's eye—no pun intended. He created them in his
image and gave them free will, the freedom to make their
own choices. Then Satan enters the picture and deceives
them by saying that God is *not* who he claims to be; Satan
implies that God is really just a jealous kill-joy who wants to
keep Adam and Eve (and by extension *us*) from realizing their
true potential. He portrays God as an insecure deity who's
afraid humans will become like him, so he has to find ways
to keep the humans down. "So don't believe him!" Satan says

to them. "Do the one thing he told you not to do, and when you do it, you'll be like him! It's your ticket to the big time, kids! You'll be enlightened and liberated! Go for it!"[2]

Q: I remember this story from Sunday school. But I don't remember Satan saying, "Go for it!"

A: I'm taking some liberties. "Go for it" is not in the actual text. Anyway, the idea that Satan is always tempting us to be "like God" has some interesting corollaries. Because that's exactly what Satan did when *he* rebelled against God's authority. He tried to take God's place, to lead a rebellion against God. And when he lost that battle, he knew that the one way to get to God was by trying to lead God's children away in precisely the same fashion, with the same bogus promise that we could "be as gods." It was a losing strategy when Satan employed it for himself and his rebel angels, and it was still a losing strategy when Adam and Eve fell for it—but fall they did.

Q: And you're saying it was all because of a lie?

A: Exactly. Of course, Satan knew it wasn't true when he said it. By this time he had already fallen from heaven, and he wanted to take as many souls with him as he could. Jesus called him the "father of lies."[3] But that's always the case with sin. It never presents itself as sin. It's always presented as a doorway to a higher consciousness, as the path to enlightenment, as the path to divinity—to becoming a god, or like God.

And in our culture, the idea of rebellion is, like, totally chic. We hardly even think about whether it's good to rebel against this or that. We just act as if rebellion is in and of itself the thing to do. People love to see themselves as rebels. Rebellion against something bad is, of course, a good thing. But rebellion against all authority is a bad thing, because some authority is hugely benevolent. For instance, God's authority. To rebel against God is like rebelling against friendship or true love. It's kind of a dumb move.

Q: **You're talking about rebellion and sin. But really, aren't most people basically good?**

A: Not according to the Bible. And yet it's important to see that God *created* us good. This requires a bit of explanation. According to the Bible, every single one of us was created in the image of God, which is all good. But there was that mysterious and bothersome event called the Fall, when our first ancestors decided to listen to Satan, who came to them in the form of a serpent. That should have been a clue right there, eh? Anyway, God's will for us was thwarted. We had the freedom to choose, and we chose poorly.

Q: **How poorly?**

A: Let's just say that every bad thing that has ever happened is a result of that single choice.

Q: Ouch.

A: Exactly. So we are fallen, and the whole Bible is the story of God trying to woo us back into the relationship humans had with him before Adam and Eve made their fatal mistake. God hasn't given up on us and won't give up on us. He loves us too much. And that's a good thing, because we desperately need him. We can't be good without him. I'm not saying there is no goodness in us whatsoever. There are flickers of it, because we are made in God's image. Goodness is there, but it's hopelessly broken. So despite good acts here and there, our nature is now ultimately self-destructive. We don't mean to be; we just are. It's as if we can't help ourselves.

Q: But any right-thinking person wants to do good, and does his or her best to do good.

A: Of course. But it's as if we're cut flowers. We might look great, but we are dying. We've been cut off from the Source. And he wants to reattach us so that his life can flow through us again. But many people say, "Hey, I'm looking great! Check out the color of my petals! The bees are all over me!" But because we're cut flowers, it's only a matter of time until we wither and die. It's inevitable. Without God, we have no life, no goodness that lasts. We were meant to live forever, but until God reattaches us to him—until we choose to allow him to do that—we have no eternal life.

Q: What do you mean when you say that Adam and Eve were created in God's image. What does that mean?

A: It means a lot of things. For one, it means that we can create—we have the ability to be creative and to create things
that didn't previously exist. But we can't create *ex nihilo,* "out
of nothing." Only God can do that, and it seems that he did
it at the "big bang" or at some point in the past when he
brought everything that exists into being out of nothing.

> It's as if we're cut flowers. We might look great,
> but we are dying. We've been cut off from
> the Source. And he wants to reattach us so that
> his life can flow through us again.

Q: **You really believe that God brought the entire
cosmos into being out of absolutely nothing?**

A: Yep. And there wasn't time, matter, or even space to work
with. No elbow room to create the entire universe! It's a
little bit like baking a cake in a really small closet, only infinitely worse. Space grew out of nonspace. It boggles the
mind. But even atheistic scientists will tell you this: At some
point the universe just exploded into existence, and it
started out as something infinitely tinier than the period at
the end of this sentence. Imagine something that small containing the entire universe. Including parts of Queens and
Staten Island. And the Jersey shore. All those Camaros!

Q: **So God can create out of nothing, but we can't?**

A: Right. We can make things out of other things, but we can't
create matter. You can try all you want, but it's not going to

happen. But we *can* create, and really, who is to say where creative ideas come from? They sort of come out of nowhere. But scientists are talking about the material universe when they say that it was made out of nothing.

Q: **How else are we created in God's image?**

A: We have the freedom to make our own choices. We have free will. Our lives and actions are not predetermined. God didn't just wind up the universe and then sit back and watch everything unfold according to some prearranged mechanical plan. He gave us the freedom to do what we like. We can reject God and choose to hate him, or we can accept him and love him. And while this is a great thing, it's also sort of scary, because having the liberty to do something doesn't mean we have the license to do it.

Q: **What do you mean by that?**

A: Having free will means we can choose the wrong thing. God won't stop us. He tries to guide us to do what is right, but he won't *force* us to do what is right.

Q: **So I could choose to wear the paisley shirt I get all the compliments on, and that's good. But I could also choose to wear it with the plaid pants, and that's bad.**

A: Something like that.

Q: **Okay, how else are we made in God's image?**

A: Well, we are persons, and God is a Person. He's not just an energy force that hums and twinkles and pulses like the

Force in *Star Wars*. He's not some Cosmic Groove that we try to get in tune with, like feng shui or what have you. He is a Person who communicates with us and has a mind that understands everything and has a will. He is the one who spoke to Adam and Eve and to Abraham and Moses and who is still speaking to people today. And he listens to us when we talk to him.

This is important: God is not the same as the universe. He created the universe, but he stands apart from the universe. In fact, he stands apart from all space and time. But he is a Person, and when Jesus' disciples asked to see God the Father, Jesus said to them that if they saw him (Jesus), they also saw the Father, so we know that God is a Person. But that doesn't mean we can explain it or understand it entirely.

Q: So just being a person means I'm made in God's image?

A: Yes, which is nothing to sneeze at, and it should give anyone with self-esteem issues pause. God's view of us, of who we are, is staggering, and since he is infinitely wise and since he made us, he should know. The Bible says that we are "fearfully and wonderfully made."[4] It also says that when we are with God in heaven, we will sit in judgment over angels, which is pretty mind-boggling.[5] It's hard to fathom how extraordinary we ordinary mortals are when you see what God thinks about us. And, oh yes, we are immortal too. Forgot about that.

Q: You're telling me that because we are made in God's image we are immortal?

A: Right; we will never die. Of course, where we exist for eternity is up to us, but we will never die. We weren't designed to die. We were designed to live with God forever amid all the unfathomable joys and glories the Bible describes. C. S. Lewis, in his famous essay "The Weight of Glory," said that none of us has ever met a mere mortal. His words are always better than mine, so let me quote him. He observed,

There are no ordinary people. You have never talked to a mere mortal. Nations, cultures, arts, civilizations—these are mortal, and their life is to ours as the life of a gnat. But it is immortals whom we joke with, work with, marry, snub, and exploit.[6]

Lewis went on to say that whether we choose to avoid God entirely and become ghastly monsters for eternity or whether we choose to open our hearts to God and let him make us more and more like him, we will never die. We will exist forever in the state we choose. So, yes, we are immortal.

And because we are made in God's image and are persons and are immortal creatures, we are sacred.

Q: Right, but some of us are more sacred than others.

A: No, not in God's eyes. Being made in God's image means that while we are on this earth and the hope exists that we will choose to live with him for eternity, we are sacred creatures. Our sacredness is by dint of our being made in God's image, not because of what we do or don't do or how well or badly we behave. What we do or don't do can lead us away from God and his plan for us, but while we are still here on earth, we must treat others—and ourselves—as sacred creatures made by God. In his estimation, we are sacred and bear his divine image, every single one of us. So when we are told to love one another, there are some very good reasons.

Q: So you're saying that because we are made in God's image, we are inherently sacred?

A: Right. Good people and bad people, tall people and short people, lovable people and unlovable people, all are created by God in his image and are beloved by him and are therefore sacred and must be treated with respect and dignity because he demands it. That's where we get the idea that an unborn child has rights or that a patient in a comatose, vegetative state has rights or that an infirm elderly person has rights. Even a murderer or a terrorist has rights. Every human being has certain inalienable rights, as the Declaration of Independence put it, and those rights come from God.

No matter what one thinks of how God created us, the idea that we have been created in his image is staggering. It's hard to fathom the significance of that. If we could for a moment catch a glimpse of how awesome God really is, we would be undone. But to think that he— the infinitely loving and infinitely wise and all-knowing Creator of the entire universe—made us in his image! What can it mean? We are glorious, God-breathed creatures, created by God to love him forever.

11

Does Hell Really Exist?

What Hell Looks Like; Where It Is; Who Ends Up There

H ave you ever fallen into a manhole? Most people would answer
no, but alas, I don't have that luxury. That's because in the fall
(no pun intended) of 1985, I was walking with friends along the main
street of Middletown, Connecticut (ironically, the widest main street
in America), when I was very suddenly and violently disoriented. It's
rather hard to describe instant plummeting, but it's definitely an un-
pleasant feeling. Then just as suddenly, I was sucker-punched—
whomp!—back to reality as my arms involuntarily caught me from
going all the way down the hole.

It took a moment for my brain to catch up with my body. I was
up to my armpits in sidewalk, staring at my friends' ankles. My new
abbreviated height was a bit startling for me, and for my friends, who
no doubt regarded me as a sawed-off buffoon as I continued to talk.

Some construction workers had forgotten to replace a manhole
cover. Had my heavy winter coat and my arms not arrested my
descent, I would likely have cracked my head on the sharp metal rim
on the way down. In truth, I might have died. All of which got me
thinking for a number of weeks and months afterward... Could I not

take a sidewalk for granted? Did I now have to worry that there were holes in the very ground upon which I walked? What was the foundation of reality? Did it have one?

The point of this strange-but-true story is that just as I took the sidewalk for granted, perhaps we sometimes take God's grace for granted. We figure things can't get too much worse than they are here on earth, but we don't realize that while we are here, God's grace is all around us. We can't imagine it being removed any more than we can imagine there being a sudden absence of sidewalk. But falling through that manhole like some silent-film comedian, I began to wonder. Perhaps the happy situation we take for granted in this life does have something to do with God's grace, with his presence everywhere. Perhaps if that were removed, we'd all fall someplace. Perhaps our armpits would stop us. Perhaps they wouldn't...

Q: Do you really believe that hell exists?

A: As a matter of fact, yes.

Q: If God is supposed to be so loving, how could he send people to hell?

A: God doesn't send people to hell.

Q: Who does that? Santa Claus?

A: Um, I hate to be the one to tell you, but Santa Claus is just a projection of our subconscious need for a father figure in a red suit who gives us toys...

Q: Very funny. Seriously, though, if God doesn't send us to hell, who does?

A: Well, God is in charge of running the universe, but he doesn't send anyone to hell. The Bible says that God will do anything and everything to keep us *out* of hell, to save us. But he respects our free will, so he can't force us to accept his help. If we really want to resist God's love, he is forced to let us go. And so, in effect, we are free to choose to send ourselves to hell. Which is a scary thought.

Q: But isn't he still ultimately responsible? Why would God set it up that way, so that we could actually end up going to hell? Wouldn't God, being God, have been able to set up a universe where no one went to hell? If he's God, you'd think that wouldn't have been beyond his abilities.

A: It looks bad, doesn't it? But that's the big mystery, and we'll never fully understand it. And it will always gnaw at us to some extent, because we so deeply want to know the answer to this mystery. But really the best we can do to understand it is to see that there is something about the nature of reality that says that in order for love to exist, the possibility of rejecting that love also has to exist, and the logical extension of that rejection is hell. One way to describe hell is to say that it's a state of existence that is completely devoid of love and all the things we associate with love.

Here's another way to think of it. Love requires a relationship, and relationships are never unilateral. If I tell someone I love him or her and that person chooses not to reciprocate in any way, there is nothing there; there's no relationship. One person alone expressing love for someone else does not constitute a relationship. It has to go both ways.

Of course, we've all heard about those people who are a little wacky and who love someone who doesn't know they exist, and they *imagine* a relationship with that person. But those people usually end up being stalkers.

> For love to exist, the possibility of rejecting that love also has to exist, and the logical extension of that rejection is hell.

Q: Not a good thing.

A: No. So God can't force us to have a relationship with him; it has to be reciprocated. We have to choose to love him back. But we also have the option of ignoring him or rejecting his love. And the logical and eternal extension of that rejection is what we commonly call hell. Just as the logical and eternal extension of accepting God's love is what we call heaven, or paradise.

Q: So what exactly is hell?

A: Well, the truth is, we don't know exactly, but we do know that it's real, that it exists. As to its exact nature, we can speculate reasonably far, but only so far. We know that it's a condition or place in which we are utterly removed from the presence of God, where we are completely free of him. But again, the idea is that we have chosen this—God doesn't choose it for us. He wants us to be with him forever. But if we desire to be outside of his presence forever, we get to have our way, and the place we go is called hell.

Q: **You're saying that hell is a state of separation from God, but that's pretty vague. What about the flames and sulfur and pitchforks?**

A: It seems really doubtful that there are pitchforks. Of course, if you really really hate them, they *might* be there. But I'm not sure why hell should feature farm implements. Seriously, most of the images we have come to associate with hell are made up; they don't come directly out of the Bible or any faith tradition. The idea of a devil with cloven hooves and a tail—and who looks vaguely like Snidely Whiplash—is pure fiction. The personification of evil must be something so horrible that we would never ever want to look at it or picture it. It must make our nightmares look like pleasant dreams in comparison. So as a way of pushing this horrible idea aside, some people have turned the whole thing into a cartoon, complete with the proverbial imps and stalactites and stalagmites. I think the reality is beyond our picturing.

Q: **Can't you at least <u>try</u> to provide a description?**

A: Okay, but this stuff is real, and believe me, it's not a pretty picture. When Jesus referred to hell, he talked about a place of agony and suffering. He said, "There will be weeping and gnashing of teeth."[1]

This is too horrible to contemplate, but we really should contemplate it, because it's real. We are talking about a place of eternal death, of absolute lovelessness, of demonic horrors. Imagine a place where there is not the slightest trace of love or comfort or goodness or beauty or freedom or justice. As they say, we don't want to go there. We joke about it, but that's because it's so infinitely hideous we *have* to joke about it to deal with it. But it's no joke. It's the worst thing ever, *literally.*

Q: I think I'm getting the picture. But if you believe hell exists, where is it exactly?

A: Do you want me to give you the exact exit on the Jersey Turnpike?

Q: Then it **is** in New Jersey!

A: I was kidding. Just because hell exists doesn't mean it's a physical place, any more than heaven is. People often talk about hell and heaven as though they can be located on a map. They say "up there" for heaven and "down there" for hell. "Up there" implies clouds and blue skies, and "down there" implies stalagmites and stalactites and volcanic activity. But these are just images we've used to help us envision these places.

But just because something isn't physical doesn't mean it's not real! And I'm not talking about love and hope and joy, which are all real but not physical. This is not semantic trickery. I'm talking about actual things and places. For example, angels are not physical and God is not physical, but they exist as much as we do.

So, yes, hell exists.

Q: And you're positive it's not in Jersey.

A: Talk to me privately later.

The French philosopher Jean-Paul Sartre once famously said that hell is other people. I can't forget hearing that for the first time in college. It was at once wildly misanthropic, monstrously arrogant, and somehow also laughably pretentious. Of course, Sartre is entitled to his opinion; on the other hand, that's not the sort of comment that gets you invited to a lot of parties. But the question remains: Is hell a state of mind or an actual place, or is it, in fact, a fiction designed to get us to behave nicely while we're still in this life?

One thing I know: I fell through a manhole on the widest main street in all of America, the one with more cement and asphalt than any other. I managed somehow to find the one place where the sidewalk was missing, and it opened my eyes, at least a little bit.

12

What About Heaven?

What Happens When You Die; What Heaven Is;
Who Ends Up There

O ne Easter Sunday I was at a restaurant with my family, waiting
to be seated. A woman was in the lounge playing piano, and
suddenly she started singing John Lennon's "Imagine." I love the sound
of the song, but the irony of the lyrics on Easter Sunday was a bit
startling.

"Imagine there's no heaven," she sang, "it's easy if you try…"[1]
Here we were decked out in our springtime pastels, celebrating how
Jesus made it possible for us all to join him in heaven, while this
woman was warbling about what a downer heaven was. It was sort
of hilarious. But given the way we think of heaven today, who can
blame her?

Q: Since you believe in hell, I assume you also believe
in the existence of heaven.
A: Correct.

Q: **But won't heaven be boring?**

A: Not a chance. Without question, it will be filled with adventure.

Q: **If that's true, it would be awesome.**

A: It is awesome. Literally. But just as with hell, the depictions of heaven that we pick up on television or in the movies are a far cry from the reality. If the Bible is to be taken seriously, heaven will be something so real and so wonderful that it will make life on this planet look like the dullest, most pleasureless existence imaginable—which is one reason it's so hard to depict heaven. It's easier to show what hell might look like because that's degraded reality; all you have to do is magnify and amplify what we know of evil on earth. But how do you depict a reality that is far more glorious and exciting than the most wonderful parts of the world we inhabit? For us, it's impossible.

Q: **But what about all the angels and harps? That seems boring to me.**

A: The idea of everyone floating around on clouds with harps is nonsense. It may be hard to believe, but there is absolutely nothing in the Bible about that. We've all been taken in. Bamboozled.

Q: **Bamboozled?**

A: Yes. The images of Saint Peter at the Pearly Gates holding a ledger, like some nightclub bouncer checking to see if you're on the list, and angels on clouds playing harps…

well, it's all just a bunch of images that have been invented over the years, and somehow they get stuck in the popular imagination, and before you know it, there are *New Yorker* cartoons and dumb jokes, and it's pretty much accepted as the gospel truth. But as I've said, the reality is infinitely more exciting.

Q: So what does heaven <u>really</u> look like?

A: C. S. Lewis said that the world we live in now is a pale version of what we are to expect in the next. These are the "Shadowlands," he said, in comparison with the glories of paradise. Heaven will be everything wonderful we can imagine, and much more than we can imagine. But because it's so far beyond our ability to imagine heaven, we come up with gaga ideas of floating around on clouds with angels' wings, and, frankly, who *wouldn't* be bored by that? The truth is, we won't even *have* wings.

> Because it's so far beyond our ability to imagine heaven, we come up with gaga ideas of floating around on clouds with angels' wings, and, frankly, who wouldn't be bored by that?

Q: You're kidding, right? We have to have wings. I was really looking forward to getting a pair.

A: I'm sorry, but we just won't have wings. It's another common misconception that when we die we will become angels and have wings. But it's just not the case. Remember that when Jesus rose from the dead, he didn't have wings.

And on the Mount of Transfiguration, when Moses and Elijah appeared with Jesus, they didn't have wings either.[2] They were just humans, in their resurrected bodies. That's what scripture says happens to us. We might conceivably be able to fly, though, if that's any consolation. But the wing thing is a definite no-go. I'm really sorry.

Q: So how does a person get to heaven?

A: That's a big question. The answer is complicated, but the simple version is that we can't get to heaven.

Q: We <u>can't</u> get to heaven?

A: Bingo.

Q: So what do we do?

A: *We* can't get there, but God can *bring us there.*

Q: This sounds like a matter of semantics.

A: Okay, consider this analogy. You're on the coast of California, and you want to swim to Hawaii. No human can make it. The worst swimmer in the world and the best swimmer in the world have exactly the same chance. Both will drown long before they even get close to making it to the shores of Hawaii.

But some people don't see it that way. They are still comparing themselves to others rather than looking at the overall goal. They'll say, "Look, that guy only swam a hundred yards, but I can swim a mile!" Someone else will say, "I can swim ten miles!" The best swimmer in the world can swim something like a hundred miles. But Hawaii is so much farther away that no one even comes close. And getting there isn't graded on a curve. It's literally sink or swim. You either make it or you don't. And guess what? No one makes it. Getting to heaven is just like that.

Q: No one gets to heaven?

A: Not under their own power they don't.

Q: So how does anyone get there?

A: God comes and gets us. He can swim the distance, and he can carry you, no problem. Or, if he needs to, he can move Hawaii closer to California. But no matter how you slice it, he can take care of the problem.

Q: Okay, so how does God take care of the problem? Wait, let me guess. The person who swims the hardest, regardless of ability—that's the one he comes and saves, right?

A: No.

Q: It has to be that.

A: Well, you're right that it doesn't depend on our talent or abilities. But in your scenario, it would still imply that our efforts to be good get us into heaven. That if I try really hard, God will be impressed. So the idea is that by trying very hard, we can impress God, and impress our way into heaven. But trying to impress him doesn't work. Well, actually, there *is* one way we can impress God.

Q: How?

A: By not trying to impress him.

Q: Sounds paradoxical.

A: It is. Truth is fundamentally paradoxical in many ways, isn't it? But it's true: The one thing we can do that will get God to come and get us is to simply say, "I can't make it. Will you please come get me? Help!"

Q: A cry for help? That's it?

A: Basically. Remember the thief on the cross next to Jesus? He simply said, "Lord, remember me when You come into Your kingdom." And Jesus replied, "I say to you, today you will be with Me in Paradise."[3]

When we admit we need God, he sees that we really get it, that we finally realize no matter how hard we try, we *can't* get there on our own. So we ask him to get us there. It's by humbling ourselves, really. It's just the opposite of boasting about how hard we're trying and what fine people we are. It's saying that without God, I'm a moral failure and I need his help, and I'm not ashamed to admit it.

Q: So God is impressed by humility?

A: By *real* humility. Remember, human beings can fake anything, and we often try to fool God by acting humble or by doing things that look extremely humble, while all along in our hearts we are saying, "Look at me, how humble I am! I'm way more humble than anyone else!"

Q: **I get the idea. But to be honest with you, I don't think I've ever seen anyone do what you just described.**

A: Sure you have. Almost every time people tell you how hard they pray or how much they read the Bible or how much they help others, they are telling you they are morally superior to you. And there are people, like ascetics, who do it in a big way, by flagellating themselves until they are bloody or by crawling miles and miles on their knees in some sort of pilgrimage. Inside they very well might be thinking, *Look at what a wonderfully humble person I am!* But God looks at the heart. He is God, and that means he is never fooled. Ever. So why try?

Q: **What happens when you die?**

A: Well, it depends, but typically the lawn goes unmowed for a while, and the newspapers really pile up…

Q: **Again with the joking.**

A: Sorry. Okay, seriously, according to the Bible, when you die, you face God and his judgment. And either you are welcomed into God's glorious presence for eternity (a.k.a. heaven) or you are banished from his presence for eternity (a.k.a. hell).[4] Is that serious enough for you?

Q: I'd have to say it is.

A: The idea that there is a judgment—that what we've done in our lives has eternal consequences—is not a very popular idea, but it's clearly what the Bible says, and it's what Christians of every stripe have taught and believed for the past two thousand years. It's obviously what Jesus believed and taught.

Q: Jesus talked about this?

A: Absolutely. In fact, what Jesus had to say on the subject was about as harsh as it gets. In case you think Jesus was some wan, smiley, mild-mannered, spiritual waif patting kids on the head and giving everyone a free pass for their self-serving behavior, let me give you a few choice quotes from the gospel of Matthew. Jesus was referring to himself here:

When the Son of Man comes in His glory,...then He will sit on the throne of His glory. All the nations will be gathered before Him, and He will separate them one from another, as a shepherd divides his sheep from the goats. And He will set the sheep on His right hand, but the goats on the left. Then the King will say to those on His right hand, "Come, you blessed of My Father, inherit the kingdom prepared for you from the foundation of the world.... Then He will also say to those on the left hand, "Depart from Me, you cursed, into the everlasting fire prepared for the devil and his angels...." And these will go away into everlasting punishment, but the righteous into eternal life.[5]

Q: Well, you're right. Jesus is no Caspar Milquetoast.

A: Right. We're definitely not graded on a curve.

The sentiment behind John Lennon's "Imagine" would make a lot of sense if heaven didn't actually exist. But not only is heaven real, it is ultimate reality. It's reality the way God intended it to be, with total freedom and total peace and joy and love. That's why our troubles here are nothing when we compare them with what God has in store for us in eternity. Not that we shouldn't try to make things on earth wonderful and peaceful in the meantime. We should and we must. But still, the idea of a paradise in this life only carries us so far. Eighty or a hundred years on earth with no wars and everybody loving one another would be glorious, but then what? We still have to leave this world eventually. And at that point, heaven might look like a very attractive possibility.

13

Why Are Religious People Such Fanatics?

*Forms of Fanaticism; The Born-Again Thing;
Christians in Your Face*

I n Manhattan, where I live, there is a man who stands on a traffic island in the middle of Park Avenue every weekday morning. He sports dirty glasses, tattered clothing, a huge unkempt beard, and a wild mane of hair. He paces back and forth, ranting and raving at the people passing and at the tall buildings on either side of him. To complete the cartoon stereotype, he waves a huge tattered Bible, and sometimes, if you're lucky, he will say something nasty about homosexuals. This is the face of religion for thousands of commuters in New York City. Is it any wonder the topic of religion is usually off limits in polite conversation?

Q: Why do so many people who take their faith seriously act weird and fanatical?

   A: You don't have to get personal...

Q: **Sorry.**

A: But I admit, you do bring up an excellent point, and the answer has several facets. First of all, many people who come to faith have been going through something traumatic and dark and hopeless, and then suddenly they see an answer, a light in the darkness, and they recognize that this is *the* answer, that God is real and it's all true, and it completely overwhelms them. They can't believe it's this wonderful, but they know that it is, and they feel that they just have to tell everyone. And often they forget that whenever you are passionate about something, you can end up sounding like a wacko on wheels.

Q: **So they're passionate converts, not fanatics?**

A: Sort of. People who've found God are often like people who have fallen in love. We've all met people who just can't stop talking about this person they've met and how wonderful that person is. They are in love and want to share it with everyone. But to people on the outside, all the gushy descriptions can be off-putting or boring or just plain annoying.

But there's another way to look at this, which is not so positive. For example, sometimes a person comes to faith, and that faith is not a real and authentic faith in the God who created the universe. It's more like instead of falling for Jesus, the person has fallen for a religious system, a way of seeing the world that is mostly a moral code. These people—who often portray themselves as people of authentic faith—are actually *not* people of authentic faith in Jesus.

But we get them mixed up with people of authentic faith. The fact is that these people are "religious" in the negative sense. They have a sense of moral superiority toward others rather than a sense of humility and awe and love.

> People who've found God are often like people who have fallen in love. They just can't stop talking about this person they've met, and it can get annoying.

Q: **Then you <u>know</u> the fanatics I'm talking about.**

  A: I've met a few, yes. It happens to a lot of people, even people whose intentions are good. It's all too easy to mix up God with "religion," and sometimes you can even have a little bit of both. On the one hand, there is the reality of an authentic faith in the living God. On the other hand, there can be a sterile moral code, which is mere "religion." But religion isn't the answer. The Bible is crystal clear on this point: God gets close to those who have been humbled by their sense of failing and reach out to him. And he opposes those who think they are so morally righteous that they are better than everyone else and don't see that they are in utter need of God's help.

     The perfect illustration of this was the Pharisees, an influential group of Jewish religious leaders in the first century. They were the most visible religious people of their day, and they were *outwardly* above everyone else, morally speaking. They made a big show of how religious and morally superior they were, implying that they were closer to God than anyone else. And yet they were the only people whom Jesus openly and severely denounced.[1]

Q: What is a "born-again" Christian? Doesn't that usually just mean a fanatic?

A: The phrase *born-again Christian* is widely misunderstood and has been abused terribly over the years. But it originally comes from the gospel of John, in which Jesus said, "Unless one is born again, he cannot see the kingdom of God."[2] Jesus was having a conversation with Nicodemus, a Jewish religious leader. Nicodemus was interested in Jesus, but he was afraid to express his interest publicly, so he met with Jesus after dark. As they talked, Jesus made the "born again" statement I just quoted. And Nicodemus, like many of us, responded by saying, "How can a man be born again? After he's left his mother's womb, that about ends the thing, no?" or something along those lines. And Jesus explained that he didn't mean being born again physically; he meant being born in a different way. He meant we need to be born "of the Spirit."

Jesus was saying that just as we are born physically into this world, we must also be born again, born into the kingdom of heaven. But we can do this while we are still on earth. We can enter the kingdom of heaven spiritually right now, even though we are physically on earth. That's what it is to be "born again."

Q: **Why do some people feel the need to call themselves "born-again Christians"?**

A: It really does seem a bit redundant. According to Jesus, any real Christian is, by definition, "born again." But I think in the 1970s people who had a profoundly life-changing experience with God started using this phrase to say that they had been, well, *profoundly* changed by an experience with God. They wanted to differentiate themselves from people who just went to church but weren't really into it very much. So they started to call themselves "born-again Christians," and from that point on, the culture began to use the term to refer to anyone who took their Christianity very seriously.

Q: **So a "born-again" Christian has had a profound religious experience?**

A: Yes. That person has been deeply changed by his or her experience with *God*—not with a mere religious system—and the person's life shows evidence of this profound encounter with God. Although it bears repeating that anyone who really is a Christian must have had his or her life deeply changed by God and is therefore a "born-again Christian," even if the person doesn't use that label. So people who take their Christian faith seriously, whose lives are different because of their faith in Jesus, are born again.

Q: **Then what is an evangelical Christian?**

A: It's sort of the same as a born-again Christian—and in most cases, it's exactly the same thing. It's someone who takes his or her faith seriously, so seriously that the person wants to share it with other people.

Q: **You mean "share" as in get up in my face and annoy me even though I have no interest in the subject?**

A: It seems to me that you have a lot of interest in the subject.

Q: **Okay, but I have no interest in hearing about it from them.**

A: Well, the people who are annoying about the way they share their faith kind of ruin it for everyone. But I don't think you want to tar everyone with the same brush. Every group has its annoying advocates, and somehow they are usually the loudest and most visible. That's just human nature. But these individuals certainly shouldn't be taken to represent the whole group.

Q: **If Jesus told his followers not to judge, why are Christians so judgmental?**

A: Christians can be awfully un-Christlike at times; there's no doubt about it. But isn't it possible that in accusing others of being judgmental, we ourselves are being judgmental?

Q: **Good point.**

A: Maybe the Christians who come across as so judgmental are having a hard time of it and are trying the best they can right now. You never know, and it's always best not to judge anyone too harshly.

Q: But we were talking about the ones who are judgmental.

A: Yes, and of course it's disappointing and sometimes infuriating to see some Christians not acting very Christlike and being judgmental. By the way, this is called hypocrisy, and God is *against* it. So anyone who knows and loves God is against it. But time and time again you'll bump into it, because in case I haven't mentioned it before, human beings are imperfect.

Also, just because someone claims to be a Christian doesn't mean he or she actually *is* a Christian. A lot of people go to church but don't have any relationship with God and don't have the foggiest idea of what it is to behave in a Christlike manner. Being a follower of Jesus and going to church aren't always the same thing.

Q: But why do most of the publicly vocal Christians come across as being so hateful? Does God hate his perceived "enemies" as much as some Christians seem to?

A: It's human nature for us to remember the anomalies, the exceptions to the rule—the hypocrites, if you will. If a Christian who appears on a televised forum or debate is thoughtful and considerate toward her opponents, we might not think much of it. But if someone who calls himself a

Christian is somehow un-Christlike in any way, we're sure to remember it, because we see it as hypocrisy, which of course it is.

Q: Exactly.

A: But television is another factor in the equation. More often than not a producer will book a somewhat outrageous guest rather than booking someone who will simply make you think more deeply. That's just the way it is, and it's unfortunate. The bottom line is that television is a business. If producers can drive "eyeballs" to their programs, as the industry lingo puts it, they're going to do that. Never mind that it isn't good for the culture and that it leads people away from being more thoughtful on the big issues that matter.

One surefire way to get people to watch your program is to book a well-known figure, some flamboyant loudmouth who is almost a parody of himself and whom you can count on to play the predictable role he's been assigned. This person can either be the outrageous and enraging conservative or the outrageous and enraging liberal. In either case these people are surefire ratings getters. But usually they are poor representatives of the people they claim to speak for.

Many devout and thoughtful Christians disagree with all kinds of things said in the name of Christianity, but they generally don't get a chance to rebut what is said, so the general public never hears it. Instead, we're stuck with a handful of high-visibility motormouths on both ends of the spectrum. Not that any of them are evil or entirely thoughtless, but they tend to merely play a role and generally muddy things up terribly rather than clarify things. And they don't come across as loving their enemies, which is the point of your question.

Q: **But aren't Christians supposed to love their enemies?**

A: Absolutely! One of the core teachings of Jesus is that his followers are to love their enemies. And anytime you stand up for something, you will have enemies. Jesus himself had them. But Christians are commanded to bless those who persecute them. And that isn't because Jesus wants his followers to lose. On the contrary, he knew that the most powerful thing in the world really *is* love. I'm not talking about mushy, romantic love, but self-sacrificial love, the kind Jesus demonstrated most radically and explicitly and famously on the cross, by dying for people who in many cases hated him. There is power in that kind of love. Loving someone who hates you can disarm them, can blow their whole way of seeing the world out of the water. They don't know how to deal with it. There is something about that kind of love that is powerful, the kind of love that gets in where nothing else will succeed. And that's because somehow people can sense that the source of this kind of love is God himself.

Q: **Are people really supposed to "turn the other cheek"? Turning the other cheek seems so wimpy. If Jesus said that, he can't really have meant it.**

A: You think turning the other cheek is wimpy? Think about Martin Luther King Jr. and the whole civil rights battle. Dr. King was a radical Christian who really believed what

Jesus taught and powerfully lived it out in his dealings with social injustice. He told his followers that they were not to fight back, that they were to "turn the other cheek" and love their enemies. He knew this was the bravest thing they could do, and he knew that loving one's neighbor and turning the other cheek is the secret power that can't be resisted, because somehow it's backed up by the power of God. It's real, and one's enemies can sense this.

When it comes to lost causes, the best and only way is always turning to God and doing what he says. In the case of Dr. King, he knew that if the marchers fought back, they'd be beaten by a superior force of policemen. But if they didn't fight back, if they did the unthinkable and loved those who persecuted them, they could win. But it takes a deep and strong faith. So Dr. King told his followers on the bus to Selma, Alabama, that if they weren't prepared to be like Jesus in this, they should get off the bus. If they weren't prepared to turn the other cheek, he didn't want them with him. That's radical Christianity, and it's real Christianity, and God honors it. It's not merely a nice idea. It's at the heart of who God is, and it has real power, world-changing power. It has God's power behind it, the power that created the universe and sustains it right now. But very few people ever have the guts to practice it, so they never find out.

Q: So you believe that loving your enemies actually works?

A: No question about it. But Jesus didn't tell his followers to love their enemies only because it works. There's more to it.

Jesus commanded his followers to love their enemies
because God loves all people, even the ones who have
drifted from him or have deliberately turned their backs
on him. It's his will that if there is any way for those who
have strayed to see the error of their ways and be brought
back to the fold, then it's worth trying. So when Jesus said,
"Do to others as you would have them do to you,"[3] he was
saying, "Put yourself in the shoes of the person who is persecuting you, who is your enemy." If you were in that person's shoes, how might someone approach you to get you to
change your position? How might someone get through to
you? If you were as blind to something as that person is,
what might conceivably get you to open your eyes and see
things differently?

Jesus tells us that by treating our enemies exactly as we
would want to be treated—in short, by loving them despite
the fact that they are totally unlovable—we might get
through to them. And even if we don't get through, we've
honored God, the one who loves them as much as he loves
us. But it's more than that. God does not want us to
become like the people who hate us. God wants us to
answer to him and his agenda, not to theirs.

The wild man thundering anger and judgment from his invisible pul-
pit in the middle of Park Avenue is not a great advertisement for God.
In fact, sometimes you have to wonder if he isn't a paid advertisement
for the other side, so to speak. But for every angry screamer like him,

there are thousands of people quietly doing the will of God. Yet most of them, cowed by the frightful image of this crazy man and his cohorts across our land, say nothing about what motivates their loving acts and their courage against injustice. Unless these people of faith know that God wants them to speak up and to present a visible, loving alternative to the screaming-meemies on street corners and cable channels, they will stay silent, afraid to bring up the very thing that everyone desperately wants to see: that God is real and that he loves everyone.

14

How Can Anyone Take the Bible Seriously?

*Religious Texts; Dinosaurs; The Big Bang;
Digging Archaeology*

In 1785 William Wilberforce, one of British Parliament's youngest members at twenty-six, had a dramatic conversion to Christianity. From that point on, his principles and actions would be formed not by what was politically expedient but by what the Bible taught. That year Wilberforce began an exceedingly unpopular campaign to abolish the slave trade in the British Empire. The odds against success can hardly be overstated. The British saw the slave trade as the lifeblood of their economy, and Wilberforce was reviled both by his peers in Parliament and by the public. But he knew what was right. And so he spent the rest of his life working tirelessly in the abolitionist cause.

At long last in 1833, nearly fifty years after Wilberforce's conversion, the loathsome institution of slavery was once and for all abolished throughout the vast British Empire. Wilberforce lived to hear the great news, and just three days later went into the presence of the one who had given him his difficult assignment. Abolitionists in the United States were inspired by this glorious victory, and three decades later they succeeded in their cause as well. Because of one man who took the Bible seriously, the world is forever changed.

Q: I agree that the Bible is valid for those who believe in it, but isn't it just one of many great religious books, like the Koran, the Bhagavad-Gita, and the Upanishads?

A: No. At least not according to the Bible itself, which might sound like circular reasoning, but it isn't.

Q: Why isn't it?

A: Because according to the Bible you have to choose between it and all other books that claim divine authorship. The Bible says that it alone is the sacred Word of God, so it logically follows that this claim is either true or it isn't. You can't have it both ways. To be logical and intellectually consistent, you have to choose between the Bible and the other sacred books.

This isn't to say that other religious texts don't have good things to say and some real wisdom to impart, but you do ultimately have to choose between the Bible and the others. There's that choosing thing again.

Q: Why do I necessarily have to choose?

A: As I've said, logic and intellectual honesty demand it. But also, God says you have to choose. In the Bible there are places where God emphatically says that we can't have it both ways. Of course, he's just forcing us to be logical and intellectually honest. But it's true, we can't have God plus any other gods we like. It's either God or the others, but not both.

Q: **Okay, but sometimes you get the idea that God is just petty and jealous. He wants to get** all **the attention.**

A: Here's a comparison that might make sense. If a guy is married and he tries to persuade his wife that he needs to have a few other women on the side, his wife will likely say, "Sorry, Romeo, but that's not going to fly. If you want to be married to me, you have to forgo those other women. Period."

It's just like that with God. He doesn't force us to pick him, but he does force us to choose between him and the others. We can't have both. Those are his conditions. He won't let us have that kind of relationship with him any more than a woman will let her husband have that kind of relationship with her. That's the deal, and we can take it or leave it. I guess you could say that a certain amount of Aretha-style R-E-S-P-E-C-T enters the equation.

Q: **Where in the Bible does it say this?**

A: Well, the Bible doesn't specifically mention Aretha Franklin, but it does point out that God *is* a jealous God, but not in the petty sense. He won't let us cheat on him. There's a famous passage from the book of Kings in the Old Testament worth mentioning.

The prophet Elijah set up a contest between Yahweh,

the God of the Jews, and Baal, the god of the pagan
nations. Elijah was begging the Israelites to make up their
minds! "How long will you falter between two opinions?"
he asked. "If the LORD [Yahweh] is God, follow Him;
but if Baal, follow him."[1] Later, Elijah got sarcastic and
mocked the prophets of Baal, wondering aloud what was
delaying their god. "Maybe he's day-dreaming or using
the toilet or traveling somewhere."[2] You don't think of
Old Testament prophets as being comedians, but that's
what he said.

Q: You're kidding again...

A: No! He really did make the toilet comment, but it has been
wrongly smoothed over in some translations of the Bible.
There are many other places in Scripture where God makes
it clear that we all have to choose, that not to choose is like
hanging out on the front lines, unable to decide which side
of the war we're on. God never says, "Hey, worship whoever
you like. I'm easy." God makes the choosing thing very
clear: The other gods are false gods, counterfeits and frauds
and pretenders to his throne. To worship them is to trust in
something untrustworthy, something that will disappoint us
and harm us and will ultimately destroy us. But God really
loves us, and he wants us to see that, to know that, and to
give ourselves to him. And doing that means we have to
show the door to all the other lowdown, no-count gods
who do not love us and never will.

Q: Okay, so the Bible claims to be the exclusive written revelation of God, and God says I have to choose either for him or against him. Besides that, what are the objective reasons that I should take the Bible seriously?

A: Just for starters—and I know this might sound incredible— there are good scientific reasons for choosing the Bible over other religious texts.

Here's an example. Look at the order of creation given in the book of Genesis. It says that the universe was created before the Earth, and the Earth was created before living beings. Life in the oceans came before life on the land, and human beings were created last of all. It's even more complex than that, and the order of it all is absolutely what science tells us it is. But Genesis was written 3,500 years ago! How would someone writing thirty-five centuries ago know any of this, about the order of creation, something we didn't know until the twentieth century? How did that happen?

Q: I admit it's something I hadn't thought about.

A: But what's really astonishing is that there's only one creation myth besides the Genesis account that comes *anywhere* close to corresponding with what we know from contemporary science, and that's the Sumerian creation myth, which gets several of the elements *out* of order. And it's likely that the Sumerian myth came from the Genesis account to begin with. But almost all of the others, and there are hundreds, sound *nothing* like it.

Take, for example, the Aztec creation myth:

The mother in the Aztec creation story was called Coatlique (the Lady of the Skirt of Snakes). She was created in the image of the unknown, decorated with skulls, snakes, and lacerated hands. There are no cracks in her body, and she is a perfect monolith (a totality of intensity and self-containment, yet her features were square and decapitated). Coatlique was first impregnated by an obsidian knife and gave birth to Coyolxanuhqui, goddess of the moon, and to a group of male offspring, who became the stars. Then one day Coatlique found a ball of feathers, which she tucked into her bosom. When she looked for it later, it was gone, at which time she realized that she was again pregnant. Her children, the moon and stars, didn't believe her story.[3]

My point is not to pick on the Aztecs. It's just one of many creation myths that all sound pretty much alike. They make nice stories, but you can't begin to see any correspondence to the scientific view of origins in them.

Q: Fair enough.

A: Despite all the noise to the contrary, the fact is that if you go through the Bible, there is nothing in it that contradicts what we know of science, as there is with other sacred texts. The God of the Bible is the God of all truth, not just "religious" truth. He is the one who created an ordered universe that we can study and understand. He is the God of mathematics and science, or he's not God at all.

We have this crazy idea that science and faith are mutually contradictory. But anyone who really believes that must have a false idea of what science is—or a false idea of what faith is. Don't buy the science-versus-faith shtick. It's just not true.

Q: **Are we supposed to believe that God literally created Adam out of the "dust of the ground"?**

A: We can't get fixated on unknowable details. Plus, what if the description is somewhat poetic? I'm not saying it definitely is, but what if it is? What if the passage means that God created humans not literally out of dust or mud, but out of the elements available on earth…and then breathed his life—his divine spirit—into this body to create the first human being? The point is, there's nothing in this that's obviously off base, as there is in almost every pagan story of human origin.

Q: **Okay, what about the dinosaurs?**

A: What about them?

Q: **Do you believe in them?**

A: Of course. But I don't believe in Barney. I just refuse to.

Q: **Okay, but if you believe dinosaurs existed, how do you account for the idea in the Bible that the world was created a few thousand years ago? Science teaches that dinosaurs roamed the earth millions of years ago.**

A: Well, for one thing, the Bible doesn't say when the universe came into being.

Q: It doesn't?

A: Absolutely not. In the seventeenth century a certain Bishop Ussher came up with a famous—or infamous—chronology that was supposedly based on the Bible. He claimed that he had pinpointed precisely when the universe was created, and it was about six thousand years earlier, like on a Tuesday at 2:00 p.m. Actually, the date was October 23, 4004 BC. That's pretty specific. Many people took him at his word, so as a result, a lot of people over the years have come to the conclusion that the Bible says the world was created six thousand years ago.

Q: But you're saying the Bible doesn't say that?

A: It doesn't. Ussher seems to have had a lot of influence, so people have treated his view as the gospel truth. But today, people who take the Bible seriously disagree over this issue. Many think the world came into being about 15 billion years ago, but this is one of those questions that isn't really resolved. If the experts can't agree on something, we can probably figure that it's not worth losing sleep over.

Q: But what do you think?

A: I honestly think there isn't enough evidence on any side to be entirely sure, and that there's solid evidence on both sides. It seems likely that the universe was created in the "big bang" about 15 billion years ago. And the age of the earth is about 4 billion years. But the more one reads about the big bang theory, the more one is convinced that if it did happen, God was the one behind it.

Q: Why do you say that?

A: Because for the entire universe to have been created in the fraction of a millionth of a second *out of nothing* is inconceivable, unless you factor in God's involvement. The idea that space itself did not exist before that is mind-bending. The universe didn't grow inside a preexisting space; it grew out of an infinite *lack* of space. Just saying that hurts my head.

From the point of view of pure physics, the moment of the big bang constitutes what physicists call a "singularity." In other words, we can trace the universe back to that moment, but not beyond that moment. So many physicists have no problem thinking that an intelligent force was behind it, but who they think the intelligent force is and who the actual God is may differ greatly. But the evidence that creation didn't just happen is increasingly compelling. Even Anthony Flew, who was one of the world's most famous and outspoken atheists, recently came around to this idea and now believes there is a God who created everything. Now that is *really* shocking.

Q: **What does the Bible say about evolution?**

A: Well, nothing specifically. It's not as if Moses gave a speech to the Israelites on Darwin's theory of natural selection. But what the Bible says by implication is worth looking at.

Q: **Such as?**

A: First of all, one thing all folks who take the Bible seriously agree on is that humans did not evolve out of nothing by accident. That is something the Bible *does* take issue with, and even Christians who on some level accept evolution can't believe in blind evolution.

Q: **What's blind evolution?**

A: It's the theory that we are here completely by accident. That life just randomly evolved out of the so-called primordial soup and that from a few proteins 4 billion years ago, we just *happened* to evolve into who we are today, right down to our ability to sculpt the *Pietà* and write *Hamlet* and construct Mars Explorers and particle accelerators and nuclear submarines. Not that I can do all those things, but you know what I mean.

Also, the second law of thermodynamics says that everything tends toward disorder or entropy. So the idea that matter would suddenly reverse direction and things would start creating themselves out of nothing is kind of far-fetched, although most of us have heard it so many times that we just assume that's the way it all happened. But it didn't. I mean, the idea of an airplane assembling itself out of scrap metal and bits of fabric and rubber and glass and plastic is patently absurd, and the idea of proteins simply assembling themselves randomly is really not very different. In fact, the latter would be far *more* complicated.

Q: You can talk all you want to about the supposed accuracy of the Bible, but isn't it true that people wrote the Bible, not God?

A: No. To be perfectly accurate, people *who were inspired by God* wrote the Bible. In other words, God is behind every word of it, and he inspired every word of it. But he didn't dictate every word of it.

The facts are that the Bible was written by about forty different people over the course of fifteen hundred years, but taken as a whole, it comes from a single point of view. That, in and of itself, is stunning. The Bible contains portions written by Moses fourteen hundred or so years before the time of Jesus, and portions written by David one thousand years before Jesus, and portions written by people who personally knew Jesus. But all sixty-six books of the Bible are of a piece and seem to fit together in exactly the same way they would if they had been written by a single author. There are themes that begin in Genesis, weave throughout the Bible, and are finally resolved in Revelation, as if a single author had been working on it all by himself.

Q: But how does anyone know what the real documents
said? No one has copies of the originals. Couldn't
they have been changed over time?

A: There is so much irrefutable historical evidence for the
scriptures being exactly the same today as they were when
they were first written that, in comparison, all the works of
ancient Greece and Rome are on very shaky ground. And
that's saying something, because historians never go around
saying that Aristotle didn't say what we think he said or that
Herodotus didn't write what we think he wrote. It's amazing, really.

Q: I'm not following you...

A: Aristotle wrote in the fourth century BC, right?

Q: Right.

A: But the earliest copies of his writing date from *over one
thousand years later*. So we have no proof that those manuscripts weren't changed dramatically from what they were
when Aristotle wrote them. But no one seriously questions
that. We just accept their accuracy.

In contrast, the New Testament scriptures were written
in the first century AD, and we have manuscripts from only
one or two hundred years after they were first written. The
time lapse between composition and the first extant manuscripts is a heartbeat in historical time. And not only that,
but most major historical documents, such as the writings
of Aristotle or Plato or Herodotus, only exist in a few old
manuscripts. With the New Testament, though, we have

literally *thousands* of manuscripts. From a literary and
historical perspective, this is almost unbelievable.

Q: **What's the point of all this?**

A: The odds of medieval monks or anyone else having mon-
keyed with anything significant in the biblical documents
are less than zero. There's a great book on this subject with
the unimaginative title *The New Testament Documents: Are
They Reliable?* written by biblical scholar F. F. Bruce. Worth
a look if you want to know more.

Q: **But what about the Old Testament? It's so much older
than the New Testament. Doesn't it stand to reason
that it was adjusted or changed over the centuries?**

A: Actually, the evidence for the continuity of the Old Testament manuscripts is similarly solid and fascinating. Just
think about the Dead Sea Scrolls. In 1948 two shepherd
boys in Palestine discovered some ratty old documents in
some pottery jars in a cave in the desert. They later came
to be known as the Dead Sea Scrolls. They were two thousand years old, and they had been untouched for twenty
centuries.

Q: **Okay...**

A: Among them was a scroll of the book of Isaiah from the
Old Testament. And when it was examined, it was precisely
the same as the book of Isaiah we have in our Bible today.
Here was hard and rather startling evidence that nothing
had been changed in all those thousands of years.

Q: But how do you know that historical references in the Bible—such as places and wars—are accurate and not just legends or folk tales?

A: Again, the evidence is overwhelming. Every time you turn around, there seems to be a new archaeological confirmation of what the Bible tells us.

For example, just a few years ago, a reference to the house of David was found on a three-thousand-year-old stele column discovered in the Middle East. Before that, historians thought that perhaps the Davidic kingdom was just a legend. And why shouldn't they assume that? Then out of the sands of Palestine, we find an ancient reference that provides hard evidence. This was reported in the *New York Times,* as most of these major discoveries are. But they just come out in dribs and drabs, so you have to keep your eyes peeled.

Another extraordinary discovery along these lines—one of my favorites—happened more than a hundred years ago in 1876. This was really the Mother of all Archaeological Finds. More than fifty times the Bible mentions a group of people called the Hittites. Uriah, the soldier whom King David had killed, was a Hittite. It seems that everywhere you look in scripture, you bump into a Hittite. But in the archaeological or historical record, there was zero evidence that these people ever existed. So in the nineteenth century, many biblical scholars used this as evidence that the Bible was largely mythical and not historical.

Q: Okay...

A: So imagine the looks on their faces when an archaeological dig in 1876 in Turkey (led by one Hugo Winckler—no relation to "the Fonz") turned up a mind-blowing number of artifacts, including a vast storeroom filled with something like ten thousand clay tablets. Because you see, once these tablets were deciphered, a significant announcement was made to the world: "The Hittites have been found!"

That archaeological site is now accepted as the capital of the Hittite Empire. Before that, many biblical scholars quite firmly assumed that the Hittites were totally made up. But now there was archaeological evidence for their existence, just as the Bible had maintained all along. And this trend toward archaeological corroboration of what the Bible says has continued ever since.

Q: Is the Bible really supposed to be taken literally?

A: Only the parts that are meant to be taken literally.

Q: Eh?

A: Well, there are many kinds of writing in the Bible, and some passages are meant to be taken literally, while others are meant to be taken metaphorically. But that's true of all writing, isn't it? When the poet William Blake wrote "Tiger, Tiger, burning bright,"[4] he didn't expect anyone to picture a flaming tiger sprinting goggle-eyed through the jungle and smelling of burnt fur, did he? He didn't mean it *literally.*

And when he wrote "Little Lamb, who made thee?"[5] he wasn't expecting the lamb to stand up, clear its throat, and say "Gaaaawwd!"

And in the Bible, when Jesus said, "I am the door,"[6] he didn't mean to imply that he was made of wood or that he swung on hinges. And when he said, "I am the vine,"[7] he didn't mean that he would sprout leaves. And when he told parables, he knew—and his hearers knew—that he was just telling stories. For example, there wasn't any actual guy in history known as the good Samaritan. These are metaphors and stories. But when we read about Moses or King Saul or King David or Bathsheba or King Solomon or Isaiah or Peter or Paul, we are reading about things that actually happened and are meant to be taken literally. They might make good stories in the same way that the story of Abraham Lincoln's life makes a good story, but they are also historically true.

> When Jesus said, "I am the door," he didn't mean to imply that he was made of wood or that he swung on hinges.

Q: But how does anyone know what to take literally and what _not_ to take literally?

A: As with many things, common sense is a good place to start. Most of the Bible is history. It was written that way, it has been read that way for centuries, and most important, Jesus read it that way. So when the Bible says this king did thus and such and this nation defeated that nation in battle, we're not meant to take it as a parable. It *actually happened.* Just because most of the stories in the Old Testament make nice stories and provide great lessons doesn't mean they didn't happen. God wants us to read biblical history in order to learn from the mistakes of others, among other things. We can learn a lot by *not* doing what many of the characters in the Bible did.

Q: But when you talk about metaphorical stories, it seems that the accounts about Noah and Jonah and even Adam would fall into that category.

A: Just because there is no archaeological evidence that cites their names in ancient tax records doesn't mean these characters didn't exist. Jesus spoke as if they did exist and as if they did accomplish the things the Bible records about them. It's hard to fathom how Jesus, who was God and knew all things, could have made a mistake or been deliberately misleading.

Q: So being a Christian means believing that Noah built an ark and put hundreds of animals on it, two by two and all that?

A: Well, first of all, it wouldn't kill you to believe this. Either it happened or it didn't. If it happened, which it seems to have, then why is it ridiculous? It might cause embarrassment to admit such a belief in certain circles, but just because it might cause embarrassment doesn't mean it didn't happen. There's vast evidence of a worldwide flood some eight or ten thousand years ago. Who knows every detail about this? We may never know. But there's more than enough evidence to make us think twice before rejecting it out of hand.

Even if science could somehow prove that Noah *didn't* exist or that he lived to be 85 years old instead of 969, it wouldn't shatter my faith. But if a scientist could prove that Jesus was never raised from the dead, then that would be a problem. The Christian faith rests on that truth, but it doesn't rest on Noah building an ark, although, based on what we can know, I still believe Noah did build the ark. My faith doesn't depend on animals in a boat, but it completely depends on the divinity of Jesus and his crucifixion and resurrection from the dead. That's a deal breaker. It's *the* deal breaker. The apostle Paul said that if Jesus hasn't been raised from the dead, everything that is taught in the Bible is meaningless.[8]

So if anyone tries to have any kind of Christian faith yet denies that Jesus was God and that he rose from the dead—in a physical body, with nail-pierced hands and feet and a pierced side—they are concocting their own version of things.

Q: **But isn't Christianity easier to believe without this idea of a bodily resurrection?**

A: Absolutely. But the problem is that without the resurrection, it would be nothing more than a collection of nice ideas about how we should live. And frankly, it would contain some untruths, too.

Why would anyone follow the teachings of a first-century rabbi who lied to us? The resurrection is one of those nonnegotiables. We can quibble over Noah or Jonah if we really want to, but the facts of Jesus' coming to earth and being born of a virgin and being crucified and raised from the dead are the bedrock of the Christian faith. Without them you can't have a Bible that makes any sense, or a faith that makes any sense. If you want to explore this further, there are a number of excellent books that get into the evidence for the resurrection. I'd start with John Stott's excellent book *Basic Christianity.*

Have you ever heard of anyone in history being imprisoned or executed for distributing copies of Grimm's fairy tales? What would you say if you'd heard that copies of *The Iliad* and *The Odyssey* had been banned in Saudi Arabia and North Korea? Imagine people trying to smuggle copies of Hans Christian Andersen's works into China? Such ideas are comical, but the Bible, which has been called a mere collection of myths and fairy tales, has suffered all of these fates. Throughout history and even today, copies of the Bible are banned and burned, and those possessing it are persecuted and imprisoned. There's something about this ancient book that threatens and frightens those in power, especially those who use power to oppress people weaker than themselves. And they have every reason to be frightened.

15

What Exactly Is Christianity?

Religion Versus Relationship; Trust Versus Belief

Not very many years ago, billionaire media mogul Ted Turner made a well-publicized comment about Christianity, calling it a "religion for losers." Many Christians were offended, but on some level his statement contains a great truth. Christianity is for people who know they can't get through life alone, who know they need help. It's not for people who believe they can do just fine on their own.

But you have to wonder which is the worse state: knowing you can't do something on your own and having to ask for help or thinking you can do it on your own and failing. You might say that one man's idea of a loser is another man's humble realist.

Q: **What is Christianity?**

A: That's another question that doesn't have a completely satisfactory answer, really, but here's a crack at it. You could say,

among other things, that Christianity is a Twelve Step program for sinners. Something like that, anyway.

Q: **You're saying that Christianity is a gigantic Sinners Anonymous group?**

A: Sort of. You admit you have a problem, then you admit that you are powerless to do anything to solve that problem, and then you turn your life over to God to solve the problem over which you are powerless. And then he does.

Q: **What exactly is the "problem" to which you're referring?**

A: Traditionally it has been called *sin,* but you don't have to call it that if you don't want to. Whatever it is, we all have it because it's transmitted via heredity. Our parents had it, and their parents had it, and on and on, back to Adam and Eve. Let's face it, we all have "issues," and we all have bottomless insecurities, and we all have deep, dark desires and secrets that would kill us if we ever let them run wild. It's the human condition. We all know we have it; otherwise, we wouldn't be looking for ways to deal with it. All religion and all psychology are humanity's attempts at dealing with it.

Q: **So, do you think other religions can deal with it?**

A: I don't think *any* religion can deal with it. Religions are our attempts at dealing with it, but they never actually succeed. They do, however, show that we know something needs to be done. It's just that religions of various kinds inevitably fail to get it done.

Q: Even Christianity?

A: Christianity without Christ, without a real knowledge of him and a relationship with him, is just another religion. And no mere religion or ritual or dogma can deal with the problem. Only God himself can deal with the problem. People can be religious, and they might intellectually subscribe to many or even all of the tenets and doctrines of their church, but in the end that can't solve the problem of the human condition. Intellectually believing isn't going to solve the problem. And performing religious activities isn't going to solve the problem. Both are important, but they don't get us there. They aren't the same as faith in God. They have the appearance of faith, but they aren't the same as faith. And God is not fooled.

> Christianity without Christ, without a real knowledge of him and a relationship with him, is just another religion.

Q: Why isn't a belief in all those things the same as faith in God?

A: Well, people who go to church and light candles and do all those sorts of things—or who go to Bible studies or talk about God a lot—are not necessarily opening their hearts up to God. Opening your heart to him and trusting him totally and letting him do what he needs to do in your life is what is necessary. If you don't give God full control over your life, you're no different than a cancer patient who spends all his time at the hospital but never allows doctors to operate or administer chemotherapy. You can use the fact that you're at a hospital to make it look as if you're dealing with the problem, but, in fact, you're hiding from it. In the best place you could ever hide, too, because most people will assume you are dealing with the problem just because you're there.

Q: But why hide?

A: People hide because they don't want to let the scalpel get near them, since deep down they probably don't trust the surgeon, and frankly, they're not so sure they have a problem that needs operating on. And even if they do admit to having some sort of problem, they know they're not as sick as all these other people who *really* need an operation.

People hide because they think they're fine. But in reality, they're just as sick as everyone else. The only difference is that the other people are getting help. Those who seek help have the guts and honesty to admit that they can't do it on their own, while the person who hides is being prideful, which is the main sin, the one that gives rise to all other sins.

As you pretend to be fine, you may very well be thinking you're better than all those other people who need help.

Q: So the church and other religious institutions are filled with people who are hiding from God?

A: It's a terrible accusation, but very sadly, it's true. Jesus talked about it more than anyone. In fact, he's the one who used the medical metaphor in describing it.[1] He saw all of these ultra-religious people (in his day most of them were called Pharisees), and he blasted them for being hypocrites, saying they were the blind leading the blind.[2] And he said he had come into the world to save those who knew they were sick, who knew they had a problem. Those who pretended they were morally perfect and wonderful, he had no use for. They were lying to themselves and ultimately lying to everyone else. And it disgusted him.

Q: **Harsh stuff.**

A: Very harsh. Except it's coming out of the mouth of the only one who would really know these things. He blasted the recognized religious leaders, saying they were like "white-washed tombs...full of dead men's bones."[3] They were pretending to have life with their religious activity, but they were actually full of death. That's what religion without God is. It's a profound offense to God. It's worse to him than anything else, because the people who are guilty of it are guilty of trying to fool him, and he doesn't take kindly to that. If we are honest about who we are and ask for his help, he will always help us. But if we try to fool him into thinking we have it all together by being "religious"—or by being self-reliant or in denial—he turns away from us in sadness and disgust. That's tough to contemplate, but Jesus' reaction to the religious hypocrites can't really be described any differently.

All through the Old Testament, there are examples of the same thing, where God was angry with his people because they persisted in trying to fool him. It broke his heart, and it still breaks his heart when people try it today. If you love someone and want more than anything for them to be well and happy, and you see them completely in denial and fooling themselves and heading in the wrong direction, you get a little upset. That's normal and healthy behavior when we love someone else, when we care. And God does care about us—a lot—in case I haven't mentioned that already.

Q: How can God care about us like that? Isn't he simply way too busy running the universe to trouble himself with my petty concerns?

A: Well, from the point of view of us human beings, yes, you'd sure think so. But in actuality, no. Absolutely not.

Q: Why not?

A: First of all, the reason it's hard for us to see that God is *not* too busy is because it's hard to conceive of who God really is. We tend to project our own way of seeing things on him, forgetting that he is so far above us and so much more powerful than we could ever imagine that running the universe and simultaneously being involved in every tiny detail of the universe is not a big deal for him. He is the Creator of the entire universe. He is simultaneously everywhere at once, and he knows everything there is to know. He has always existed, since before *time* existed. Because he also created time.

To think of God as just a really smart and really big version of ourselves is to ridiculously limit him to our human-sized conception of what he is. But that's what so many of us do. We think God is too important and too busy to bother, so, instead, we pray to angels or saints—or maybe we don't bother to pray at all.

But think about this: If God really is too important and too busy to help us, then he's not God. And since God loves each of us individually, he actually is concerned with every small detail of our lives. Jesus said that his heavenly Father keeps his eye on every single sparrow, so *how much more* will he keep his eyes on us, whom he created in his own image and whom he loves infinitely more than we can ever imagine?[4]

God is all-knowing and all-wise, so he sees us exactly as we are, and he knows how much we need him. So when we try to fool him into thinking we have things under control without his help, we fail to fool God and succeed only in fooling ourselves. Christianity is God's way of helping us see ourselves for who we are so that we might at last begin the process of becoming who we were meant to be all along.

16

What's the Point of Prayer?

Unanswered Prayers; Faith and Prayer;
Meditation and Prayer

I n her movies, the great screen beauty Greta Garbo often played a
jaded, tortured soul. And in real life she seems not to have been so
different than the roles she portrayed. The famous phrase attributed
to her, "I vant to be alone...," seems to have somewhat accurately
captured the real Garbo. She did live alone, and near the end of her
life, the paparazzi now and again captured her for the tabloids: a sad,
lonely old woman shuffling along Manhattan's sidewalks.

In a magazine article published near the time of her death, Garbo
was reported to have scoffed at the idea of prayer, saying that she
couldn't imagine what in the world people spent so much time praying about. It all seemed to her interminably boring.[1]

Q: **What is prayer?**
  A: Prayer is when people talk to God.

Q: That's it?

A: That's it! Sometimes we do it alone, and sometimes we do it in a very informal way, such as when we're in trouble and we just say, "Lord, help me!" or "God help me!" or even just "Help!" Sometimes we don't even say it aloud; we just think it, but God can hear us anyway, and that's prayer. Other times it's very formal and can be a corporate thing, as in church or at some big event when a prayer is spoken in a kind of formal language, with *thees* and *thous* and a *beseech* or two thrown in. But in either case, prayer is simply people talking to God. We're people. He's God. We talk. That's it.

Q: But how does prayer work?

A: Well, there's no question that it's a mystery. We know a lot about prayer, but we also don't know all that much. Sometimes prayers are answered very clearly. For example, someone prays that a friend will be healed, and amazingly that person *is* healed, and everyone knows it's a miracle. The doctors know it and are baffled, the patient knows it, and the patient's family and friends know it. God heard the prayer and healed the sick person.

But other times nothing at all seems to happen. And as far as praying for healing is concerned, it seems that more often than not, nothing happens. So the question is, "What happened to the prayer?" Was it not heard or just not answered? As a result of the seeming nonanswer, many people will quite reasonably assume that God doesn't answer prayers or possibly doesn't even hear them. Or worse, they assume there is no God, that we are talking to the oxygen and nitrogen in the room. Or some people will assume that there's something wrong with the person who prayed—that his prayers weren't pure or that there is some secret sin in his life that prevents his prayers from being answered. Or sometimes people will say that the people who prayed didn't have enough faith. Or that the person who was being prayed for didn't have enough faith. That's always an impossible one to argue with, because who really believes they have enough faith?

Q: **Not me.**

A: Not anybody. But let's set the record straight: How much faith did Lazarus have when Jesus raised him from the dead?

Q: **Is this a trick question? Lazarus was dead, wasn't he? So he didn't have any faith at all.**

A: Correct. So anyone who says that the person being prayed for has to have faith needs to know that that idea is unbiblical and nonsensical. A dead man can't have any faith. So it was God's grace that raised Lazarus from the dead. *God* accomplishes these things, not our "faith." If it was our great faith—or our praying in just the right way or with sufficient intensity—then whenever a prayer was answered, we'd pat ourselves on the back as though we had done it ourselves. Of course that's human nature. But God doesn't want us to do that. He wants us to thank him for answered prayers. So anyone who says someone doesn't have enough faith to be healed or to be helped by God in some way is being hurtful. It's God's love and grace that are operational, not our amazing faith or prayer skills.

Q: So then what's really going on when prayers aren't answered?

A: We can't be sure. I'm convinced that it's a number of things, though. For example, we know that many times what we pray for is contrary to God's desires for us, just as when a little kid asks for permission to please please *please* be given three chocolate sundaes instead of having to eat her dinner. The parent knows this will hurt the child and says no. From the child's point of view, it appears that the parent is against her, but the reality is just the opposite. It's because the parent loves the child that she denies the request.

And so it is with God. We ask him for something that will end up being bad for us, short term or long term or both, and he doesn't grant our wish. Sometimes years pass before we understand God's wisdom in not giving us what we wanted. Other times we never really find out. But God won't grant something that isn't in his will.

Q: That's logical, but I'm not sure I like it.

A: God is all-loving and all-knowing, so for us to want him to do something that is contrary to his will is counterproductive in the extreme. Which is why it's so important to know God, to have a relationship with him, so you know what to ask for and what not to waste your time asking for. If you just want to get what you want, without any concern for God's opinion on the matter, you should address your prayers to someone who hates you and wants to do you harm, but not to God.

Q: **That's harsh.**

A: Maybe, but it makes sense, doesn't it? I mean, if you want to hurt someone, you're not going to ask God to do it, because he loves the person. And if you want to hurt yourself, there are powers out there that will oblige you. Really. Anyway, that sort of thing isn't in the realm of prayer; it's in the realm of the occult. Which is why, as I've said, the biggest part of prayer has to do with knowing who God is—with really knowing *him*.

What could be more intimidating and more beautiful and more strange than the idea that we can talk to the God who created the universe, and that he *wants* us to talk to him? Who can fully grasp that what we have to say would be of interest to God and could even affect his actions? If there is anything in our world that is vastly underrated, prayer would have to be it.

Q: **Is meditation prayer?**

A: No. This one confuses a lot of people, and it's an important distinction. We can meditate in God's presence, and some people do that, and often it leads to prayer. They will be reading the Bible and talking to God and then thinking about what they are reading and so on. But it's really just a different kind of prayer because they are talking to God and sitting in his presence, which they've invited by talking to him.

But most meditation—at least what people usually think of as meditation—is very different from prayer and has nothing to do with God. Prayer is talking to the God of the Bible, even if we don't know his name or much about him. So when we are desperate and cry out, "Help me!" we are often talking to God, even though we may have no real knowledge of him. But the God of the Bible makes it clear that we have to beware of talking to false gods. And the Eastern idea that somehow we are gods and that getting in touch with ourselves is the same as getting in touch with God is false and really, ultimately dangerous.

Q: **Why is it dangerous?**

A: It comes from the Eastern idea that God and the universe are one and the same. This is exactly the opposite of what Judaism and Christianity teach. According to the Bible, God created the universe, but he is entirely separate from it. He may be everywhere in it, just as air may be everywhere in a room, but the air is distinct from the room. The room can have the air sucked out of it, but the room can't have the room sucked out of it. So the room and the air in the room are two separate things. And so God may be everywhere in the universe, but he is distinct from the universe. He is the Creator, and the universe is what he created. He existed before the universe, and if the universe were to end, he would exist after the universe. God and the universe are not the same thing.

So if God and the universe, which he created, are not the same thing, it also follows that God and people, whom he created, are not the same thing. We are separate beings from God. It's true that he wants to come and live inside us, *if we invite him to do so.* But he isn't automatically there. So when we pray, we are praying to him, not to the universe, and not to some deeper version of ourselves. Big difference.

That's why Eastern meditation—which has to do with getting in touch with the *self,* which Eastern religions believe is the same as God and the same as the universe—is a profoundly unbiblical idea.

> When we pray, we are praying to God, not to the universe, and not to some deeper version of ourselves.

God is separate from the universe, and he is separate from each one of us. But that doesn't mean he leaves us alone.

Those who are familiar with Greta Garbo's story have wondered, *Did she* really *want to be alone?* Or did she fear that there was no one out there—no person and no God—who might understand her and really love her? And so to protect her heart, as so many of us do when we're hurt or angry, she told whoever might be listening, "Leave me alone."

When any one of us makes that statement, it's often true that we are desperately longing for someone to ignore our pained words. What we want more than anything is for someone to wrap his or her loving arms around us and squeeze tight.

17

What Does It Take to Believe in God?

Faith and Reason; The Question of Meaning; The Definition of Trust

When I was a kid, I had a book titled *You Will Go to the Moon.* But by the time I gained possession of the book, which was handed down from a relative, Neil Armstrong had already set foot on the moon! The book described what that journey would be like, and it suggested that by the time I was a grownup, people would be going to the moon for restful weekend getaways. Of course that hasn't happened, but it was a nice idea.

But imagine for a moment that you and a group of people have been charged with the task of getting to the moon. A number of you are brilliant physicists and mathematicians and engineers and astronauts, and you have everything at your disposal to make a lunar excursion happen. But let's say that most of you don't believe the moon exists. Houston, you have a problem. If you don't believe the moon exists, you're never going to put all the pieces in place that are needed to actually get there. And the fact is, you'll never know what it's like to bounce around in a one-sixth gravity environment. Think of the fun you'll miss!

Many of us get caught up in debating whether God exists, and we never get past that question. But the goal of life isn't figuring out whether he exists; it's taking that as a given and proceeding from there. That's where the fun lies.

Q: How do you know if you believe in God?

A: That depends on what you mean by "believe in God." Because you can intellectually believe in God without trusting in him, without loving him or knowing him. For example, Satan and his demons believe that God exists,[1] but they also *hate* God. So just believing in God doesn't really mean anything. Many times people will say, "I believe in God," but it has absolutely no bearing on their lives. If they really knew who God was, they would live differently, they would put their lives in his hands. So mere intellectual belief that God exists isn't much of a big deal. If Satan and every demon in hell believe God exists, then mere intellectual assent can't mean much in a good way, can it?

Q: I never thought of it that way.

A: So those who believe in God have to go one step further and say that they *trust* in God, that they put their faith in him, that they believe he is who the Bible says he is, and that he loves them more than they can ever imagine. If you know who God is, you will want to turn your will over to him, because you trust him with your life, you trust that his plans for you are far better even than the plans you've made for yourself. But if you don't really believe that God is the loving and wonderful God of the Bible who knows you intimately and loves you passionately, you'll never feel free to trust him with your life. You'll always hang back out of fear that it's all a trick and you're being hoodwinked.

Q: **What if you can't believe because you aren't sure and don't believe you can ever be sure?**

A: Almost everything in life is a judgment call. In criminal cases in a court of law, there is a required standard of proof known as "beyond a reasonable doubt." You have to weigh the evidence and make a judgment. You aren't saying that the evidence falls completely on one side and that it's an open-and-shut case. You are weighing the evidence on both sides of the argument and ultimately making a judgment call.

We do this all the time in many areas of life. We're never 100 percent certain about anything because we couldn't possibly be. When we get in a car and turn the key, we trust that the car will work and will take us where we need to go. Some people know exactly what makes a car run, but most folks really don't have a clue. But this doesn't mean that we don't get in the car and drive places. We've made a reasonable judgment call that the car works. We don't have to understand every little thing about the car, but we know enough right now. We know what we need to know.

And this knowledge, though incomplete, is not based

on nothing. It's based on the evidence we have. We've ridden in a great variety of cars, and we've seen them work. We have no reason to doubt the evidence. Just because we don't know what a differential is, or what a universal joint is, or how an automatic transmission works, or what the technology is behind antilock disc brakes doesn't mean we don't know enough to make a good judgment about whether we can trust the car to get us to work. We know more than enough to make a wise decision, so we open the door, get in, and drive. And it's just like that with God. At some point we need to make a decision.

Q: But why do we need to make a decision? Why not simply choose not to make a decision one way or the other?

A: Because that's being intellectually dishonest. Not choosing is a kind of choosing. We are never going to know everything, and we may still have lots of questions, but the big question is whether there is more evidence on this side of the God argument or on the other side. If not knowing something makes us feel unqualified to make any kind of decision in life, we are like the guy who refuses to get in a car because he doesn't fully comprehend the internal combustion engine. We all have lives to lead, so who has the time to spend years studying motorized transportation? No sane person would be that ridiculous. We'd deny ourselves something good for no good reason.

But when it comes to God, people say that unless they can really know every little thing and solve every mystery, they won't make a decision. At the end of the day, you have to ask yourself if those people really want to make a decision. Maybe they *don't* want to make a decision, and so they use this excuse to get out of it. If someone did that with a car, you'd know they were crazy. At some point you have to get in and drive because you need to go places.

Likewise, in deciding for or against God, we have enough evidence on which to base a decision, if only we'll face up to it.

Q: **All of this requires a lot of faith. But isn't faith just an idea or a fiction?**

A: The Bible says that "faith is the substance of things hoped for, the evidence of things not seen."[2]

Q: **You just lost me.**

A: Okay, let me back up. The Greek word for faith in the New Testament is *pistis,* which really has more to do with trust than with intellectual belief. So what we have faith in is what we trust in. This applies to small things as well as large things. For example, I have faith that the chair I'm sitting on will support my weight. I put my trust in certain things, and that means I have faith in them; I trust them to do what they are designed to do.

But faith in God is no different than faith in my favorite chair. I am relying on the trustworthiness of something, based on past experience and knowledge. But for some reason, whenever people talk about faith in God, everything gets a little mushy.

For example, if you told me that you have faith that your car will start in the morning, but for the last five mornings, it hasn't started, I wouldn't say, "Hey, it's great that you have faith in your car." On the contrary, I'd say, "What's wrong with you? Your car hasn't started in five days, and nothing has changed to make it start, so your belief that it will start is pie-in-the-sky wishful thinking." And really, it's *worse* than that, because you've missed five days of work, and you'll now miss a sixth and likely get fired. You need to understand that what you believe is quite different from reality. If you believe that your car will start, you should base that belief on good evidence. Instead, you have evidence it *won't* start, and yet you believe it will. That isn't faith; that's foolishness. Believing in something that isn't true will only get you into trouble.

In the New Testament, Saint Paul said that he and the disciples didn't believe in myths and fairy tales. It's not enough that the Bible is full of nice ideas. What it says must be real and true the way history is real and true, or else we're simply kidding ourselves.

Q: **But isn't faith a leap in the dark? It's just something you either have or don't, right? You can't reason your way to faith, can you?**

A: Well, faith means having trust in something, and to trust in something that is irrational or against reality is silly. As someone once put it, "Faith isn't a leap into the dark; it's a leap into the light." Anyone who leaps into the dark might fall into an abyss, because they can't see what's out there.

God doesn't want people to trust in "whatever" and take dumb risks. He wants people to trust in him because he's utterly real and utterly trustworthy. If he isn't real and worthy of our trust, we'd be fools to have faith in him. The object of our faith must be worthy of our faith.

> If God isn't real and worthy of our trust, we'd be fools to have faith in him. The object of our faith must be worthy of our faith.

Q: Okay, here's a big question: How did we get here?

A: To this part of the book? Most people just flipped the pages.

Q: Ha. No, I meant how did we humans get to this planet?

A: Well, there are two fundamental theories on how we got here. Each one has variations, but basically there are two. The first one is that a personal Creator God, who loves us, deliberately put us here. He created the entire universe and then created us in his image and placed us in this setting that he had created specifically for us.

Q: Okay...

A: And the second theory is that there is no God, so we got here entirely by chance, which is to say, by accident. Amazingly this second theory is the prevailing view in most circles. But it has some deeply troubling aspects that you never really get to hear about—maybe because they add up to, like, the biggest bummer *ever.*

Q: **What do you mean?**

A: Simply this: If we got here by chance, it follows very logically that life has no meaning whatsoever. No. Meaning. Whatsoever. Very few people can really face up to the infinite black hole of this idea, maybe because if you really do face up to it, you'll want to just crawl under the nearest couch and hum indefinitely. The implications of complete meaninglessness are huge and nightmarish. But again, if everything that exists, including us, is a chance by-product of blind evolution, there's no other alternative. Most people try to finagle an alternative, but it just doesn't follow logically.

Q: **Here we go again with blind evolution.**

A: Yeah. As we discussed earlier, blind evolution means evolution that is not directed by God but simply happens by chance and accident over time. In other words, *we just got here.* It was not intended; it just happened, and here we are. But as I've said, the inescapable implications of this are tough to swallow, so folks who subscribe to this theory mostly just ignore the unhingingly bleak implications.

Q: **What are you getting at when you refer to these implications as being so awful?**

A: If there is no God and we got here entirely by chance, and if life has no meaning, it then follows that every beautiful feeling you or anyone else ever had—and every noble idea about love and justice and freedom—is just an unintended and random by-product of evolution and is therefore *inherently meaningless.*

Q: **That's grim.**

A: You're not kidding. The idea of an accidental universe means that, quite literally, there is no such thing as love. Or goodness or transcendence or justice. They would all be constructs that are inherently empty, that we just made up—or worse yet, that evolution accidentally programmed into us. According to the theory of blind evolution, the overwhelming, heartbreaking love that parents feel for their newborn child is nothing more than an evolutionary quirk designed to preserve the species. It has no more value than the stink gland that a skunk has to protect itself from its enemies. It's just a mechanism that evolved randomly and that perpetuates the species—but for no particular reason. That's the ghastly part. It's all for no reason. It just happened by accident.

But who can accept that, really? How many of us who have accepted the popular notion that we evolved out of nothing would be willing to take the next logical step and say that the love we have for our children or parents or friends is utterly meaningless—just a biochemical quirk put there by evolution? Almost no one can accept that for what it is. People try to weasel out of these implications, but we all have to look at the logical conclusions of our beliefs. Our beliefs should be able to withstand that kind of scrutiny, but the belief that we evolved accidentally really can't, so we tend to look away from it, to pretend it's not there.

Q: **Okay, I get the point. It's all pretty bleak.**

A: Wait, it gets bleaker! Because you'd even have to go so far as to say that your need for meaning—and the idea that you think a meaningless universe is bleak—is *also* meaningless. So somehow your need for meaning along with everything else in life is simply an evolutionary quirk. Dostoevsky said that without God, "everything is permissible." And he's right. When there is no God and, therefore, no meaning, then you can't say there is anything wrong with mass murder, for instance. It's all totally meaningless. Which is a tad depressing.

Q: **Yes, a tad.**

A: But there's great news. Actually, all of this is a powerful and logical reason to believe in God. The theory that we all got here by accident and that everything that makes life noble is actually meaningless *is not true!* It's nonsense. Kind of makes you want to take the rest of the day off and celebrate.

Remember the fictional team assembled to pull together everything needed to launch a trip to the moon? Well, let's say we've figured it all out. The moon really exists! Now what? Wasn't the original goal getting there? Are we now content to stay on the ground, simply believing that the moon is out there somewhere? Or do we want to build the rocket ship and go?

We live in a culture that treats the existence of God that way. Some folks get to the point of believing he exists and then stop there, as if that were the point. It's not. Have we figured out that God exists? Great! But that just means we've reached the starting line. Or the launching pad, if you will. Now let's take a deep breath and get ready to take off in God's direction.

18

Who Says Jesus Is God's Son?

*Jesus as More than a Moral Teacher
and a Great Role Model*

Almost everyone who was alive on July 20, 1969, remembers that day. On that day human beings from the planet Earth landed on the surface of the moon. We all remember the famous words "The *Eagle* has landed," and then those few pregnant minutes when untold millions of people held their collective breath. In those moments, there in the lunar module, two men were getting ready to step onto the cold, bleak, airless surface of the moon.

Before they emerged, there was a radio blackout so they could quietly prepare themselves for the epochal moment just ahead, when they would exit the module and change human history forever. The vast majority of people still don't know what the men were doing in those meaningful moments, but I can tell you what one of them was doing. Commander Buzz Aldrin Jr. had wanted to do something that was appropriate to the extraordinary significance of the moment. So he opened a small vial of consecrated wine and a small container of consecrated bread, and reciting the words his pastor at home had told him to say, he took Communion. Before setting foot on the moon, Aldrin took part in an ancient sacrament that commemorates the crucifixion of Jesus Christ.

Q: I'm interested in the idea of Jesus as a teacher and a role model, but things like the crucifixion have always put me off. Why do I have to also accept that Jesus is God's Son?

A: It's great to respect Jesus as a moral teacher and as a role model, but as C. S. Lewis famously put it in his book *Mere Christianity,* Jesus didn't leave that option open to us. Besides, respecting him merely as a moral teacher and a role model isn't Christianity.

Q: It's not <u>your</u> version of Christianity, maybe, but who's to say it can't be mine?

A: Everyone can believe what they want. But people can't believe whatever they want and *call it Christianity.* That's just intellectually dishonest. Christianity is Christianity. You don't have to like it, but you do have to be clear on what it is before you decide whether you like it or don't like it.

If Christianity can be said to mean whatever you want it to mean, then you can't very well complain when someone kills people and says that's *his* version of Christianity and God told him to do it. Relativism works both ways.

Q: **Isn't that a rather extreme comparison?**

A: Yes, but it's fair.

Q: **But what's wrong with thinking of Jesus as a moral teacher?**

A: Well, the idea of Jesus as a moral teacher is nice, and the world would certainly be a better place if everyone tried to behave like Jesus and do the things he taught. But it's still not Christianity. In fact, I have no idea what it is. Wait, I take that back. I know exactly what it is: It's like saying you ordered the spaghetti carbonara because you liked the smell of it, but you weren't going to eat any of it. But you insisted that smelling it was no different than eating it.

Q: **What?**

A: Spaghetti carbonara is made for eating. So everyone who eats it smells it, but not everyone who smells it eats it.

Q: **Where are you going with this?**

A: I'm saying that Jesus was a great moral teacher, but the fact that he was a great moral teacher is very much *beside* the central point of Christianity. It's like the smell of spaghetti carbonara. You might like the way it smells, but if you don't eat it, you are really missing the whole point of it, the whole *raison d'être* of the dish.

Q: **Okay, so what is the central point of Christianity? Or the "raison d'être," as you put it?**

A: The central point of Christianity is that Jesus came into this world to *save* us, to use the loaded, old-fashioned term. He came here to die on the cross and rise from the dead, thereby defeating sin and death. If he hadn't done that, then everything else he's known for—his moral teaching and even his miracles—would be meaningless. Jesus didn't come into this world to teach us how to be nice people, despite rumors to the contrary.

Q: **Why would his moral teachings be meaningless without his crucifixion and resurrection?**

A: Because his *main* moral teaching was that we need *saving*. In other words, he came to teach us and show us that we can't be good without God's help.

Q: **Why can't we be good without God's help?**

A: Think of what Jesus taught. He agreed with the Hebrew scriptures that adultery was a huge sin. But then he went much further and said that to merely lust after a woman was the same as committing adultery with her in your heart. Who can live up to that sort of standard?

Q: **I can't think of anyone right this minute...**

A: *No one* can live up to that standard. Not that we shouldn't try, but the point was to say that we all will fail, and therefore we all *desperately* need God's help and mercy. The point of Jesus' moral teaching was not that we should simply try harder. It was to make us understand that we need God. That's the beginning of all wisdom.[1] Until we ask him to come into our lives and help us, we are basically kidding ourselves.

Q: **Kidding ourselves in what sense?**

A: In the sense that we are not admitting our true moral condition. It's like a guy in a prison cell who thinks that all his problems would be solved if someone would just come in and give the cell a fresh coat of paint—and maybe bring him a more comfortable mattress. But he won't or can't admit he's a prisoner. Or he doesn't understand that he's a prisoner and that what he *really* needs is to be let out of his cell.[2]

Q: **So you're saying we're prisoners? Isn't that going a little overboard?**

A: It is if it's not true. But we need to know that whether or not we agree, that is the one thing Jesus was trying to get across to us. He was saying that he has the keys to free us from our prison. All we have to do is ask. But that's very difficult for us to admit. So we say, "Um, just give me a coat of fresh paint, and I'll be fine. Maybe a mattress, too. But I'm fine, really. No, really…"

Q: **Isn't the idea that we're prisoners of sin just a guilt trip, not to mention incredibly negative?**

A: It's extremely negative. What could be more negative than the idea that we are condemned prisoners, unable to help ourselves? But once we see where we stand—at least where we stand in Jesus' estimation—we are able to say, "Okay, I'd like to get out of here. I'd like to be free." And he frees us. That's the whole point of who he is. So it's initially negative, but it's only when we see the negative part—that we need God—that we are able to accept the hopeful and glorious part—that God wants to meet our need and does when we ask him to.

Q: You make it sound so easy.

A: On the one hand, it is, but first you have to admit that you're a prisoner, which is *not* so easy.

Q: But why is believing we are prisoners, or lost and in need of saving, so difficult?

A: Pride. Our pride is a huge obstacle to seeing who we are in God's eyes. We desperately want to see ourselves as self-sufficient. We want to do it our way, without help, without owing anybody. That's human nature.

But there's no way around it. On this one, we need God's help. Period. And we can't accept his help unless we accept Jesus and what he did for us on the cross. That's the free gift of salvation. Once we accept that gift, we are free to receive his help in being a better person. But if we want his help only so that we can be better people, but refuse to accept him as the Messiah who died to reconcile us to God, we're missing it all. We're smelling the spaghetti carbonara and saying that's the same as eating it. People who think like that will starve. And not only will they starve, but they'll also miss out on the unbelievable taste of spaghetti carbonara.

Q: So you are convinced that Jesus was divine?

A: Do you mean divine as in "simply marvelous"?

Q: Ha. No, I mean it literally, as in "God."

A: Well, yes, he was.

Q: Why do you have to believe that a human Jesus was and is God?

A: We know that Jesus was indeed a real flesh-and-blood historical figure, every bit as real as Alexander the Great or Shakespeare or Ben Franklin. He lived and died, and through his actions and words, he had a greater effect on our world than any historical figure who ever lived. But he was much more than that.

  The Bible doesn't teach merely that Jesus had godlike abilities, or that he expressed God's thoughts, or that he did God's will, but that he actually *was* God, the one who created the universe and time and space, the one who is the Author of all life (including yours and mine and all of our ancestors), and without whom neither we nor anything else would exist. No one, including Aristotle and Chaucer and Napoleon and Eli Whitney and Mahatma Gandhi, can claim the same.

Q: I guess I don't understand why Jesus' divinity is so important. Why push that aspect of it?

A: The main reason his divinity is important for Christians is because it's true. The claim of the Bible and of all orthodox Christians throughout the ages is not simply that this is what we believe or that this is how we see him, but that this is what is actually true, as true as the fact that the earth is round and gold is an element and one and one make two.

But if it were merely a matter of opinion, then we would be fools to believe it, and that's an important distinction to make, because sometimes people act as if religion is a matter of opinion when in most cases it's not. You can hate Jesus or you can love him, but when you die you'll discover the absolute truth of who he is, no matter how you feel about that truth. Our feelings about his divinity or lack of same don't change the reality of it. So that's the first reason it's important to Christians: because it's actually true.

But another reason it's important is because if Jesus was merely a moral teacher and a great role model, then the rest of his life didn't make sense. If he thought he was God and claimed to be God and actually was not God, why would we bother with his moral teachings? He'd be a madman or a liar, and who would listen to what he had to say? And yes, he did claim to be God.[3]

It's also very clear that the men and women around Jesus, who were his close friends and followers, saw him this way too. They knew him and believed that he was God in the flesh. So we're sort of stuck. We have to choose to accept him as God or reject him as a madman or a liar. There's no other logical alternative.

Q: **What's all the fuss about the blood of Jesus? Why in the world is a bodily fluid so central to the Christian faith?**

A: Well, sure, if you don't have any context, the concept is completely weird. But the context is everything. First of all, in ancient Hebrew culture—and in almost all of the cultures of the world—blood is sacred. The ancient Israelites saw blood as the embodiment of life itself, and of course, to a large extent we basically see it that way today. But for the Israelites, blood *was* life. So when we talk about the blood of Jesus, we are really talking about the very life of Jesus.

> If Jesus claimed to be God and actually was not God,
> why would we bother with his moral teachings?

Q: **I'm with you so far...**

A: And since Jesus is God, he is sinless and perfect, so his blood—his life—is perfect too.

Q: **You're saying his blood somehow represents his perfection?**

A: Exactly. So one way or the other, by choosing Jesus, by giving him our hearts and our lives, we effectively trade our blood for his. So we trade our sinful, broken, unrighteous lives for his sinless, perfect, righteous life. He takes on our sinfulness and brokenness and unrighteousness—and the spiritual death that results from them. And we take on his sinlessness and perfection and righteousness—and the spiritual life that results from them. Jesus, who shouldn't have died, died in our place. And we, who should have died, live because we can have his life in us.

Q: **Not a bad deal, if I may say so. But exactly why does God do this?**

A: Because he loves us, and that's what true love is, sacrificing yourself for the object of your love. And, of course, the sacrifice of Jesus was the ultimate sacrifice, a sacrifice we can't entirely understand.

Q: **But why do we deserve this great sacrifice on his part?**

A: That's just it. We *don't* deserve it. Which is what makes it all the more amazing. It is pure grace and pure love. It's not something we've earned or can ever earn. To try to earn God's love is to miss the point entirely. He loves us already. We can't be more loved by him. So to try is like adding numbers to infinity. You can't get higher than infinity, and his love for us is infinite.

Q: **If that's the case, then why should anyone even try to be good?**

A: Why, indeed? We should try to be good out of gratitude to God. It is the only proper response. His love for us is so vast and limitless and heartbreakingly beautiful that when we finally see it, we can't help but love him back. We can't help but want to please him. Our gratitude wants to express itself, and that's how it expresses itself—by seeking to please God.

So people we might call saints are not those who have earned their way into God's good graces by performing good acts. Saints are those who know they are unworthy of God's love but see that he has loved them anyway. And once they see this, they are so moved by his grace that they spend the rest of their lives doing good by sharing God's grace with others.

God always loves us first, and then we respond. To try to earn his love is silly and pointless. He already loves us more than we can ever imagine. He only wants us to see this, no matter what hopeless situation we might be in. Because once we see it, we'll begin to change.

It's interesting to think that some of the first words ever spoken on the surface of the moon were those of Jesus: "I am the vine, you are the branches. [Whoever] abides in Me…[will bring forth] much fruit."[4] Astronaut Buzz Aldrin said that he'd intended to read this communion passage in his transmission back to earth, but at the time, NASA was embroiled in a legal battle with Madalyn Murray O'Hair, the outspoken atheist who was suing NASA because the *Apollo 8* crew had read a few scriptures from Genesis when they orbited the moon on Christmas of 1968. Aldrin had been asked not to read the scriptures over the radio, and he reluctantly complied, reading them quietly as he gave thanks to God.

"It was interesting for me to think," he said some years later, "the very first liquid ever poured on the moon, and the very first food eaten there, were the communion elements."[5] And interesting for us to think that the first symbolic act on the moon was a remembrance of a self-sacrificial act of grace made two thousand years earlier by the one who made the moon and the Earth and the stars.

19

Jesus Isn't *Really* the Only Way to God, Is He?

The Path to God; How God Reveals Himself

The outrageous specificity of Jesus is counterintuitive. If God is the Creator of the universe and of every single person on our planet, why would he choose to reveal himself mainly through a thirty-year-old Jewish man at a particular time in history—and long before the world's population was connected through mass communication? What exactly could God have intended by doing things that way?

Q: Isn't it ridiculously arrogant to say there is only one way to God? Or, to be more specific, to say that Jesus is the only way to God? What about all the people who have never heard about Jesus?

A: This is *the* classic question.

Q: I thought you said earlier that the one question about a good God allowing human suffering was the classic question.

A: Well, they're *both* classic questions. But as far as this one goes, the Bible tells us over and over that God looks on the heart. So he is concerned with things like humility and relying completely on him, not with our intellectual and theological knowledge. And in the New Testament we learn that God can use his creation to reveal himself to people, which leaves us all without an excuse.[1] We can't plead ignorance, whether we know the name of Jesus or not. So it seems that a person can respond to God without necessarily knowing all the biblical teachings about him. But in North America, where we hear about Jesus over and over, we don't have to rely on God's creation to find out who God is.

Q: We don't?

A: No, we have the life and teachings of Jesus to reveal God to us. But either way, it's absolutely vital that we understand that God longs to have a relationship with us. He's not looking to trick us or trip us up. A pagan god might do that. They are always portrayed as being mischievous and tricky because they are made by humans and reflect human flaws and weaknesses. But God isn't like that. He is fairness and justice itself.

But still, this whole question misses something.

Q: What does it miss?

A: It puts the whole thing negatively, which is to say, backwards. God isn't trying to cast people into hell; he's trying to bring them into heaven. He wants people to be with him and to have everything his sons and daughters should have. So it's odd to focus on the question of whether people need to hear the name *Jesus* to go to heaven, as if knowing him in this life were an annoyance people would prefer to avoid.

It's just the opposite. Knowing Jesus and knowing all about him are meant to be monumental blessings in *this* life. So we should be tripping over ourselves to get to know him rather than trying to figure out ways people might get to heaven *without* him. People's lives here and now will be infinitely better if they know Jesus and the freedom he wants them to have.

> God isn't trying to cast people into hell;
> he's trying to bring them into heaven.

Q: Why are Christians so hung up on the idea of salvation?

A: Well, it's not just Christians who have this hang-up. The idea of salvation actually goes back to Old Testament times, to the moment God announced himself to a pagan nomad named Abram and told him to leave his home country and go to a land God would eventually reveal to him. Over hundreds of years, God created a nation out of Abram's descendants. That nation was made up of Hebrew slaves who were set free from Egypt and became the nation of Israel, God's chosen people.

Q: So you're saying that you believe the Jews are God's chosen people?

A: Yes. That's what the Bible says, and that's what Jesus believed.

Q: Why would God play favorites like that? What makes the Jews so special?

A: It does seem unfair in a way. And like many things, it's not something we can totally understand. But we can know that the whole reason God chose Israel was specifically to reach everyone else—to reach all the other nations in the world.

The word *heathen* that we see in scripture simply means "nations," so that all the nations other than Israel were called "heathen." God's plan was to use Israel as a way to reach all of those other nations that had no knowledge of him and were still worshiping pagan gods. But being God's chosen people is a burden. For Israel to be the nation through which God would reach the world is no small thing. Who would deny that it has come with terrible suffering as well?

But why did God choose Israel and not some other nation? I don't know. I do know that the whole plan of God's saving the world has everything to do with Israel. It's his story. He wrote it, and we have to accept it.

Q: Since we're on the subject, what exactly is that story?

A: The story goes like this. God created Adam and Eve in his image, to be his children forever. They blew it—big understatement—and wandered off on their own, away from

God and his love. It caused them and their descendants endless suffering, and it broke God's heart. So the rest of the Bible is basically the story of God wooing us back.

Q: **What do you mean God wants to "woo us back"? Woo is not a verb I hear every day.**

A: It implies an abiding love, which is the case between God and his people. To get on with the story, God had to start somewhere. First he had to introduce himself to one person, and that person was Abram (later renamed Abraham), circa 1900 BC. Before God visited Abraham, Abraham was just a pagan, worshiping false gods like everyone else. But God introduced himself and said that he would make Abraham the father of a great nation. And so all of Abraham's descendants became the nation of Israel. And God's plan all along was to use Israel to be a light to the rest of the world, the nation that would open the eyes of other people to God.

Q: **But how would that be done?**

A: Through God's Messiah. God prepared one nation of people to know him and love him, and history shows that Israel wasn't always faithful. But God chose the Jews and stuck by them and promised that out of them he would bring his Messiah. And his Messiah would be the way the whole world would learn about God.

Q: **What does <u>Messiah</u> mean?**

A: It means "anointed one," the one God has chosen and specially prepared to do his work. The Hebrew word is

Moschiach, and the Greek version of the word is *Christos,* which we translate as "Christ." So Jesus Christ simply means "Jesus, God's Anointed One." Christ isn't Jesus' last name, in case you were wondering.

Q: Thanks for clearing that up. So you are saying that Jesus was the Jewish Messiah?

A: Yes. And because of Jesus, much of the world now worships the God of Israel. Each person on the planet who calls him- or herself a Christian of one stripe or another is following the God who was introduced to the nations via the Jewish Messiah—who came out of the nation that came from Abraham, to whom God had introduced himself nineteen hundred years earlier.

Q: So the plan worked?

A: So far, so good.

As the Bible says, God's ways are not our ways.[2] We can never know exactly why he goes about things as he does. But despite his sometimes mysterious ways, we can know that God wants us—wants *everyone*—to find him.

20

What Makes Conversion Real?

The True Meaning of "Conversion";
What Happens Afterward

I t seems that for every story about Christian conversion improving someone's behavior, there are two or three in which the converted person doesn't seem to improve much at all. A woman once said to the famous English novelist Evelyn Waugh: "Mr. Waugh, you say such horrible things to people.... How can you behave as you do, and still remain a Christian?"

"Madam," Waugh replied, "I may be all the things you say. But believe me, were it not for my religion, I would scarcely be a human being."[1] Faith does not necessarily make us perfect, but perhaps it does have a way of making us more aware of our failings.

Q: What does it mean to be **"saved"**? I find that term extremely off-putting, by the way.

A: Well, yes. The word *saved* is one of those religious terms that at this point in history has lost most of its real meaning and has merely become an off-putting us-versus-them kind of burr under our collective cultural saddle. But on some level, it's a great word, and we need to make an attempt to see it in that light.

Q: **What's so great about it?**

A: Well, it refers to the fact that we need saving. Of course, the question is, "What do we need saving from?" And the answer is, from ourselves and our self-destructive tendencies. We need help. God offers to help us, and if we accept his offer of help, we are "saved."

Q: **What is conversion?**

A: Conversion is a number of things, but on one level, it's when someone fundamentally changes his or her relationship to the world by entering a covenant relationship with God. You convert from being outside a relationship with God to being inside a relationship with him. You convert from being at a distance from God's love to being swallowed up in it.

In a way, it's like marriage. One moment you are single; the next you are married, part of something bigger than yourself. There is no in-between state; it's one or the other. For a vivid picture of conversion, think about the archetypal conversion story, the apostle Paul's so-called Damascus Road Experience.

Q: Okay, what is a Damascus Road Experience?

A: It sounds like a fancy ice-cream sundae, doesn't it? I'll have the Damascus Road Experience with extra fudge and two spoons, please. But seriously, here's the story: Saint Paul was originally a devout anti-Christian—and of course he wasn't called Saint Paul at that time. In fact, he wasn't even called Paul. His name was Saul, and he was a zealous Pharisee (a devout religious leader of the Jews during Jesus' time). Saul strongly opposed the new sect made up of those who followed Jesus; he considered them heretics and persecuted them with everything he had. In fact, he was present at the stoning of Stephen, the first Christian martyr. Saul was one of the leaders who approved of the stoning.[2] So we're not talking about some mere philosophical difference here.

Anyway, Saul was on his way to the city of Damascus carrying warrants for the arrest of any Christians he discovered there, when a blindingly bright light came upon him from the sky and literally knocked him off his horse or donkey. A voice from heaven said, "Saul, Saul, why are you persecuting Me?" Saul knew it was God and said, "Who are You, Lord?"[3] Which is a strange question, kind of like saying, "What's your name, Bob?" Somehow Saul knew that he knew who it was, and yet he didn't really know who it was. And in response God said, "I am Jesus, whom you are persecuting."[4]

Can you imagine what that sounded like to Saul? God knocked him off his high horse—literally and figuratively—and told him that he was profoundly mistaken. That would take the starch out of any zealot, wouldn't it? To have God speak directly to you and straighten you out like that?

Q: **It might have something of a sobering effect.**

A: So one moment Saul was proceeding in a certain direction, cocksure of himself and his mission, and then—*bang!*—he was stopped dead in his tracks and corrected. And he did a complete about-face. For the rest of his life he proceeded in the exact opposite direction from the one he'd been taking up to that point. He was powerfully humbled in the process, so his passion and zeal were still there, but they were now different too. Anyway, that was the original Damascus Road Experience.

Q: **You say conversion is doing a complete about-face. But a friend of mine accepted Jesus in a prayer some years ago and felt absolutely nothing. Since then his life hasn't changed at all. Aren't you supposed to feel something?**

A: People's experiences with God are as different as people are, and people are as different as fingerprints or snowflakes. Of course, fingerprints and snowflakes still look like fingerprints and snowflakes. Each is unique but still readily recognizable as what it is. Likewise, everyone's experiences with God are unique, but God is always God. He isn't whoever we want him to be. So he's always God, but each of us will experience him somewhat differently.

Q: **How are you supposed to feel when you pray to ask Jesus into your life?**

A: People usually expect some bolt of lightning because someone told them that was his or her experience, and then when it doesn't happen, they are disappointed. But it's usually *not* a bolt of lightning.

Still, some people experience something dramatic and immediate. I can think of several examples. One friend actually felt his sins being purged out of his body physically—whatever that must feel like—and then he felt the Spirit of God coming into his body. It was a very physical thing. Another friend immediately felt a deep and very palpable sense of well-being. Another friend said it was as if everything looked brighter and in richer colors for a while, and it felt as if she was just floating for several days.

Some people instantly knew they could not continue to do certain things they had done before, and they had no desire to do them. Some people have had addictions vanish, just like that. So, yes, many times people feel all kinds of things, and there is something palpably miraculous that happens. But for every one of those, there are others who say they didn't really feel much of anything.

But the lack of any special feeling really doesn't mean anything. It's sort of like getting married. Some people have a wedding that feels positively magical to them, and other people just sort of sleepwalk through the experience. But each of them is just as married as the other. You aren't less married if you don't feel married. You either say the vows and get married or you don't. The feeling is a bit beside the point—not that excitement isn't a nice thing, but it's definitely beside the main point.

Q: **Okay, but that's marriage. You know whether or not you're married. But this is a little different. There are no priests or ministers or justices of the peace, and there's no wedding license and no blood tests. So how do you know if the prayer worked?**

A: There are a number of things to consider. First of all, God is always present, and if the prayer was real by his standards, it's real and it happened. But you want to know how we can know for sure.

> God isn't whoever we want him to be.
> So he's always God, but each of us will experience him somewhat differently.

Q: **Right.**

A: Well, if a person sincerely meant the prayer, if he or she sincerely asked Jesus to come in and be Lord of his or her life, the prayer worked. Just because the person didn't feel anything doesn't really come into it, as I've said. But sincerely saying those words and meaning them is no different than saying "I do" at the altar. You can pretend nothing happened, but something happened. God heard the prayer, and as far as he is concerned, you have accepted Jesus. And when you invite him into your heart and mean it, he comes in. But sometimes time passes, and people feel nothing and see no change, and they begin wondering if maybe they weren't sincere.

Q: Exactly. I've known people who prayed that prayer at one time or another, and nothing earthshaking happened, and then they slowly slid off into a life where God was clearly not front and center. So if the prayer worked, what happened?

A: First of all, sometimes people pray the prayer, but either they really don't mean it or they don't really know exactly what they are praying. For example, they might be doing it almost superstitiously, as when someone says, "Hey, pray this magic prayer, and good things will start happening." At that point, praying the prayer to ask Jesus into your life is not very different from a chain letter or chain e-mail. It's just pure nonsense, really, and it has nothing to do with the awesome and wonderful and loving and holy God of the universe. It's as powerless as a rabbit's foot or a lucky penny.

Here's another thing that can happen. Sometimes people understand what they are praying, and they really do mean it. But there is no follow-up. In other words, if someone had told them that now that they've prayed this prayer, they need to do X, Y, and Z to learn to faithfully follow God, they would do it. But no one tells them anything, and before you know it, they are confused again and doing the same things they always did.

Q: So are there things you're supposed to do after
    you pray the prayer? The prayer itself isn't
    enough?

A: It's not that the prayer isn't enough; it's simply a matter of
    being practical. Again, it's no different than getting married.
    You can get married and mean it, but just imagine if the
    very next day you start acting like you are not married and
    go off and live with someone other than your spouse. You
    are just as married no matter what you do. But what you're
    doing is the sort of thing that might eventually end your
    marriage—or make it of no consequence in your life, which
    is almost the same as ending it.

Q: So what are you supposed to do after the prayer?
    What's the X, Y, and Z to which you referred?

A: There's nothing set in stone, but what Christians through
    the ages have said is remarkably similar. First, you should
    get involved in a church. Find a solid, "Bible-believing"
    church and begin attending and becoming part of it.
    Second, read the Bible every day and pray every day. And
    third, begin telling other people about your newfound
    faith.

    Evangelist Billy Graham always told this to everyone
    who found Jesus at his huge stadium events. He knew
    that if someone made a heartfelt commitment to Jesus but
    just walked away afterward without any plan for follow-
    through, chances were very good that the whole thing
    would end up feeling like an emotional thing that had no
    bearing on reality past the day it happened. So it was crucial

for the person to immediately do something to confirm the
faith commitment he or she just made.

Q: Okay, but these three things bring up other questions. For example, why do I have to worship God in a church? Why can't I commune with the Almighty on the beach or out in the woods?

A: Why *not* worship him in a church?

Q: Isn't God supposed to be everywhere? That being the case, isn't nature's beauty ten times as indicative of God as any church building?

A: Well, I've seen a few of the church buildings I think you're referring to, and, yes, I think any pile of sand or any random grouping of trees is more aesthetically pleasing. And, yes, God *is* everywhere, and we *can* worship him anywhere, but let's be honest. Isn't this question really just a way of trying to get out of going to church? And isn't it true that when you *don't* go to church, you don't exactly go to the woods or the beach to worship God but rather just stay at home and putter around?

Q: How did you know that?

A: Just a hunch.

Q: Okay, but that's not what I was getting at.

A: Well, seriously, there is some validity to the idea that God isn't necessarily any more present in some churches than outdoors. Still, that misses the larger point.

Q: Then what _is_ the larger point?

A: The point is that God really is everywhere, but worshiping him with other people is an integral part of a person's relationship with him. Just because God is everywhere doesn't mean we shouldn't worship him in specific places that are set apart for worshiping him with other people.

Q: Why?

A: Because community is hugely important. Traditionally, when people go off on their own, they can get some pretty wacky ideas that end up having nothing to do with who God really is but instead have to do with who they _want_ God to be. Your Jim Joneses and David Koreshes fall in that category. They go off on their own and invent their own religion, adding whatever they want and subtracting whatever they want. And the next thing you know, they effectively declare themselves God, and the FBI gets involved, and Kool-Aid is on the menu.

Q: Aren't you exaggerating a little bit?

A: Yes, but only to make the point that if God isn't the one talking to us, we are in big trouble. And other people who are part of a longstanding faith tradition, have a relationship with God, and know the Bible reasonably well can help us figure out when something is God or not. And often when we insist on going off alone, we open ourselves up to things that are _not_ God but are, in fact, the worst parts of ourselves, which we mistake for God, because there is no one around to tell us we are steering toward the rocks.

So if you are on your own, you might end up worshiping something that is not God, or you might end up believing something that isn't true. By being in an emotionally healthy community of believers, you have the benefit of checks and balances.

Q: **Since you insist on this church thing, how does a person know which church to attend?**

A: It's important to know that there's no such thing as a perfect church. As the saying goes, if you find one, don't join it, because you'll ruin it.

Q: **Ha.**

A: Churches are made up of people who aren't perfect, as you already know. So don't look for a perfect church! There's always something you won't like or someone you won't like. (By the way, this question is a great reason to read C. S. Lewis's *Screwtape Letters,* which is a hilarious and incredibly accurate depiction of what happens to many people right after they make a commitment to God.)

But just because there's no such thing as a perfect church doesn't mean there's no difference between a good church and a bad church. A good church is one that has a vibrant, faith-filled community where the people actually believe what the Bible says and what the church teaches, and they make a serious attempt to live according to those teachings. That's not really too much to ask, but there are many, many churches where that's just not the case, and I would avoid them. But even sometimes in churches that aren't all that wonderful, you can find a small group, perhaps a Bible-study group or some other group, where the whole thing is very much alive, and sometimes that's enough, even if the larger church is kind of yawny.

Q: Do you have any particular denominations in mind?

A: Not really. There are great and terrible churches in every denomination. For example, some Roman Catholic churches are filled with people who know and love Jesus and read the Bible, and you can obviously see God at work in their lives. But other Catholic churches are spiritually dead, with everybody just going through the motions. The same is true of many Eastern Orthodox churches and the churches in every Protestant denomination. Some are spiritually alive, and others are just keeping alive a religious tradition. But as I said, sometimes even the "dead" churches will have a small group of people for whom the whole thing is very real. You have to play it by ear.

But you *must* be around a group of people—even if the group is small—who know what it is to be a Christian and who are excited about Jesus and living out their faith in him. Those are the folks you want to be with—folks who have a vibrancy and joy about knowing God and following him. Those are the people who will help you grow in your faith. Probably the easiest way to solve this problem is to find a church that's offering the Alpha Course, a ten-week course on the basics of the Christian faith. That's normally a good introduction to a great group of people along the lines I've just described.

Q: You mentioned that the second thing—the Y element— was to read the Bible. How should I read the Bible?

A: You can and should read the Bible in many ways. But the best way to read it is as God's word to you, personally. Now you have to use common sense here. There are many portions of the Bible that don't lend themselves to that. But many times God will speak to you quietly, through the Bible, if you are reading it with an expectant heart—believing that God wants to speak to you. So many times while you are reading the Bible, you may have a palpable sense that something you are reading is something God is saying directly to you. The Bible is a living book, really, not just a dry historical book. God wants to speak to us through it, and we should always read it with that expectation.

Q: Can you give me an example of how this might work?

A: Sure. Let's say you are reading Psalms, which, by the way, is a book you should probably dip into every day. Reading a psalm or two or three a day is a great idea. Anyway, you may come to a passage, such as Psalm 46:10, which says, "Be still, and know that I am God." Now that's a message for everyone at all times, but sometimes it's exactly what you needed to hear right then. That's not a perfect example, but you just kind of know it when it happens. At that moment you sense God communicating to you.

Everyone who wants to have a real and life-changing

relationship with God should set aside time every day to get alone and read the Bible and pray. Usually folks do that in the morning; otherwise the day tends to crowd in, and it's harder to focus on God. But it's very important to have time alone with God where you tell him what's on your heart, what you're worried about, and what you need his help and guidance with. And it's very important that you get to know the Bible.

It's also great to use a book containing daily devotionals, such as *My Utmost for His Highest* by Oswald Chambers or a Bible that is divided up into daily readings. You can find those at any Christian bookstore or usually at any large bookstore. But at a Christian bookstore, someone can help you find exactly what would be right for you.

Q: How else should we read the Bible?

A: Read it with other people. Find time every week or so to read the Bible with others in some kind of Bible study. This is very important, because we need context on how to interpret some of what we're reading. We need to know how Christians for two thousand years have been reading the scriptures. Otherwise, we're liable to come up with a wrongheaded interpretation. History is littered with breakaway sects that have redefined parts of Scripture in ways that other Christians know is way off. There is always that temptation, so we need to read the Bible with others who can be trusted to interpret it sanely and with some sense of historical perspective.

Q: And there was a third thing, right? The Z element?

A: The third thing, traditionally, is to tell others about your
newfound faith.

Q: Why should I do that?

A: Somehow the whole thing becomes more real for you when
you share it with others. If you keep your faith to yourself,
there can be a strange tendency to begin wondering if you
ever really prayed that prayer at all. It's as if you got married
and then never again referred to your spouse or the wedding ceremony. Your faith has to become part of who you
are outside of your head, otherwise it will atrophy.

When you put your trust in God through his Son,
Jesus, you've taken an important and amazing step. Definitely let others know about it! Of course, you want to do
this sensitively, but it's better to share your faith less than
perfectly than to never say anything about it. Just be yourself and talk about what you've experienced. You don't have
to be an expert; you just have to talk about what you've
been through and what it means to you. You don't have to
do this with everyone you meet, but find a few people with
whom you think it would be appropriate. It can be an
extraordinary experience.

Another reason for talking about your faith is that
when Jesus comes into your life, you are hugely blessed—

and you need to share that blessing with others. He blesses us so that we might then bless others. Other people deserve to know about God as much as you do, and many people are hungry to hear about a person's faith journey. Many people are aching to meet someone who has had a real experience with God. They will be grateful to you if you are humble and sensitive as you share your experience with them. Good news should be shared.

Conversion to faith in God is one of the great mysteries. The signs of conversion are difficult to pinpoint, but one of them is this: Many of those who have experienced it seem now and again to have a curious and a distracted look, as though they've glimpsed something so beautiful they can never forget it, as though they've glimpsed the thing behind all things. And they have, and now they are turned toward it forever, toward that glorious faraway country that is their true home.

Appendix

Recommended Reading

Q: **I'd be willing to read more about the various arguments for Christianity. What can you recommend that is not annoying, boring, or embarrassing?**

A: There are a handful of genuinely great books, depending on your taste and what exactly you're interested in reading.

For sheer Christian apologetics, I'd first try *More Than a Carpenter* by Josh McDowell, or John Stott's *Basic Christianity*. And who can argue with C. S. Lewis's classic *Mere Christianity*? Not I. Lewis is the king of all apologists, and anything by him is worth the bother. If you're feeling a bit ambitious, there's Josh McDowell's *Evidence That Demands a Verdict*.

If you're feeling slightly literary, don't miss G. K. Chesterton's *Orthodoxy*—short and sweet *and* tart. And if you're feeling slightly more literary, read Thomas Howard's glorious book *Chance or the Dance?* It gets my vote as one of the best books of the twentieth century, hands down.

On the scientific side of things, almost anything by

Hugh Ross or Gerald Schroeder is great. Schroeder is wonderfully readable as he brilliantly discusses the way the Bible
and science not only don't contradict each other but actually complement each other. Sir John Polkinghorne is a bit
tougher to read, but exceedingly brilliant. If you feel like
wading into the evolution controversy, you could try
Michael Behe's *Darwin's Black Box* or Phillip Johnson's
Darwin on Trial or William Dembski's *Uncommon Dissent.*

If you're interested in Christian worldview, read Nancy
Pearcey and Charles Colson's *How Now Shall We Live?* Or
Nancy Pearcey's *Total Truth.* Charles Colson's *Loving God*
is also fantastic. And if you're wondering what to do with
your life, you must read Os Guinness's *The Call.* *

I could go on, but I won't. Happy reading!

---

* For further updates to this resource list, please visit www.ericmetaxas.com.

Notes

Chapter 1

1. Genesis 1:27.
2. See Matthew 9:5-6; 14:22-31; 15:16; Mark 8:14-21.

Chapter 3

1. For more on the story of Sodom and Gomorrah, see Genesis 18:20-32; 19:24. The implication is that even though God took very seriously Abraham's plea to spare the cities if they contained just ten righteous inhabitants, that many righteous people could not be found. For a dramatic example of Moses pleading with God to spare the Israelites, and God changing his mind and withholding his judgment, see Exodus 32:9-14.

Chapter 4

1. Walter Wink, *Unmasking the Powers: The Invisible Forces That Determine Human Existence* (Philadelphia: Augsburg Fortress, 1986), 1.
2. See Revelation 12:3-4,7-12; Luke 10:17-18; Matthew 25:41; 2 Peter 2:4; Jude 6.
3. John Milton, *Paradise Lost,* bk. 1, st. 8, line 22.
4. Pink Floyd, "Wish You Were Here," copyright © 1975 by Pink Floyd Music Publishers Ltd.
5. See Proverbs 16:18; 29:23.

6. Satan is described as being disguised as an "angel of light" in 2 Corinthians 11:14. Jesus described him as the "father of lies" in John 8:44 (NIV).

Chapter 5

1. 1 Peter 5:8.
2. See Luke 22:31.
3. See 1 Peter 5:8.
4. See Revelation 12:10.
5. For more on this, see the book *Hostage to the Devil* by Malachi Martin (San Francisco: HarperSanFrancisco, 1992). Another book that deals convincingly with the demonic realm is M. Scott Peck's *People of the Lie* (New York: Simon & Schuster, 1998). Those who read it won't soon forget it. Peck also wrote *Glimpses of the Devil* (New York: Simon & Schuster, 2005), a book that goes into detail about two exorcisms he was involved in.
6. See Hebrews 9:27.
7. See Isaiah 47:12-14; 2 Chronicles 33:6; Revelation 9:20-21.
8. For more details on how planet Earth is designed to support life, see www.reasons.org.

Chapter 6

1. William Blake (1757–1827), "The Garden of Love." Public domain.
2. John 10:10.

Chapter 7

1. Genesis 1:27.

2. For the complete story on these three incidents, see John 4:4-27; 12:1-3; Matthew 28:8-10.

Chapter 8

1. See Luke 11:39,42-44,46.
2. Luke 11:2.

Chapter 9

1. For more on this idea, see God's statement in Jeremiah 29:11-13, in which he promises to reveal himself to honest seekers who pursue him wholeheartedly.

Chapter 10

1. Genesis 3:6, NIV.
2. See Genesis 3:1-7.
3. John 8:44, NIV.
4. Psalm 139:14, NIV.
5. See 1 Corinthians 6:2-3.
6. C. S. Lewis, *The Weight of Glory: And Other Addresses,* rev. ed. (New York: HarperCollins, 1980).

Chapter 11

1. Luke 13:28. See also Mark 9:44,46,48, where Jesus quoted Isaiah 66:24 in describing hell as a place where "their worm does not die, and their fire is not quenched."

Chapter 12

1. John Lennon, "Imagine," copyright © 1971 by John Lennon. Administered by Yoko Ono.

2. See Matthew 17:1-3.

3. Luke 23:42-43.

4. See Matthew 7:18-23; 25:31-33,41-46; Luke 13:23-30.

5. Matthew 25:31-34,41,46.

Chapter 13

1. See Matthew 23:23-33.

2. John 3:3.

3. Luke 6:31, NIV.

Chapter 14

1. 1 Kings 18:21.

2. 1 Kings 18:27, CEV. The *English Standard Version* of the Bible translates the same verse: "Either he [Baal] is musing, or he is relieving himself, or he is on a journey."

3. The Aztec creation myth, excerpted from www.dreamscape .com/morgana/miranda.htm.

4. William Blake, "The Tyger," *Songs of Innocence and of Experience* (London: Oxford University Press, 1967), line 1, www .rc.umd.edu/rchs/rime/tygerlamb.html.

5. William Blake, "The Lamb," *Songs of Innocence and of Experience,* line 1, www.rc.umd.edu/rchs/rime/tygerlamb.html.

6. John 10:9.

7. John 15:5.

8. See 1 Corinthians 15:14.

Chapter 15

1. See Luke 5:31.

2. See Matthew 23:24.

3. Matthew 23:27.

4. See Matthew 6:26-27; 10:29.

Chapter 16

1. Source unknown.

Chapter 17

1. See James 2:19.

2. Hebrews 11:1.

Chapter 18

1. See John 15:5; Proverbs 9:10.

2. Reinhardt Bonnke (speech, New Canaan Society, St. Paul's Church, Darien, CT, May 21, 2004).

3. See John 4:25-26, in which Jesus claims to be the promised Messiah; and John 8:58, where Jesus stated that before Abraham existed, "I AM," thus appropriating the name of God for himself.

4. John 15:5.

5. Buzz Aldrin, *Men from Earth* (New York: Bantam, 1989), quoted in Bill Carrell, "Communion on the Moon—Buzz Aldrin," www.geocities.com/saved_by_grace.geo/apologetics/communion.html (accessed June 23, 2005). I met Buzz Aldrin recently and asked him about his experiences on the moon. He seemed surprised that I knew this story.

Chapter 19

1. For more on this idea, see Romans 1:18-20.

2. See Isaiah 55:8-9.

Chapter 20

1. Evelyn Waugh, quoted in Paul Johnson, "The Necessity for Christianity," *Truth Journal,* www.leaderu.com/truth/1truth08 .html (accessed June 23, 2005).

2. See Acts 6:8-12; 7:57–8:1.

3. Acts 9:4-5.

4. Acts 9:5.

About the Author

ERIC METAXAS is the author of thirty award-winning children's books, including the bestseller *Squanto and the Miracle of Thanksgiving.* He has also worked as a writer for VeggieTales videos. His humorous essays have appeared in the *New York Times* and the *Atlantic Monthly,* and while at Yale he edited the *Yale Record,* the nation's oldest college humor magazine. He currently hosts Socrates in the City, the acclaimed Manhattan speakers' series on "life, God, and other small topics."

Eric resides in New York City with his wife and daughter. For more information, please visit www.ericmetaxas.com.